W9-AZR-535

Z E N
BUDDHISM
IN THE
2OTH
CENTURY

ZEN
BUDDHISM
IN THE
2 0TH
CENTURY

HEINRICH DUMOULIN

TRANSLATED AND ADAPTED FROM
THE GERMAN BY JOSEPH S. O'LEARY

NEW YORK WEATHERHILL TOKYO

First edition, 1992

Second printing, 1995

Published by Weatherhill, Inc.
420 Madison Avenue, 15th Floor
New York, New York 10017

© 1992 by Heinrich Dumoulin.
Originally published in 1990 under the title *Zen im 20 Jahrhundert*,
by Kösel-Verlag GmbH & Co.

Printed in the U.S.A.

Library of Congress Cataloging in Publication Data
Dumoulin, Heinrich.
    [Zen im 20. Jahrhundert. English]
    Zen Buddhism in the 20th century/Heinrich Dumoulin; translated
    by Joseph O'Leary.—1st ed.
         p.   cm.
    Translation of: Zen im 20. Jahrhundert.
    Includes bibliographical references.
    ISBN 0-8348-0247-3: $14.95
    1. Zen Buddhism—History—20th century. I. Title. II. Title:
  Zen Buddhism in the twentieth century.
  BQ9262.8.D8613 1992
294.3'927'0904--dc20
                         91-47049
                         CIP

ISBN 0-8348-0247-3

CONTENTS

Introduction

ZEN
YESTERDAY
AND TODAY

Implanted in the polymorphous religion of the Buddha, confined for centuries to a narrow area, treasured and practiced by an elite, only in the epochal turning point of our times has Zen won prestige and wide influence as a spiritual force of worldwide significance. In the last decades, many unnoticed and sometimes unknown aspects of the Zen experience have come to the fore, and the uncommonly rich spiritual culture born from Zen has claimed new territory in a global outreach. The twentieth century will have marked an epochal shift in the history of Zen. The picture that emerges when we compare the Zen of yesterday with that of today is one of both continuity and change. A thorough knowledge of the roots and historical development of Zen is thus no less requisite than an openness to new perspectives.

Let us recall that the word *Zen* is the Japanese equivalent of the Sanskrit *dhyāna*, meaning "concentration" or, more widely, "meditation," namely, the meditation of Mahāyāna Buddhism. The word takes its concrete meaning from being combined with other terms, and when it is used without these in the following text, it is shorthand for either a concrete historical designation—Zen Buddhism—or a concrete activity—Zen meditation. Other historical designations include Zen school, Zen sect, Zen line, and Zen tradition, and other designations of concrete activities or experiences include Zen practice, Zen praxis, Zen koans, Zen experience, and Zen enlightenment. Expressions covering a wider realm have multiplied—Zen art, Zen culture, Zen research, the spirit of Zen, Zen philosophy—all comprehensively united under the rubric of the Zen way. But one can scarcely speak of Zen in itself, as a floating entity not tied to any of the above specific meanings. In the New Age movement, something of this sort has been attempted, but the result is unconvincing and fails to make clear the nature of such a Zen above and outside Buddhism and all concrete specifications.

Zen comes from Asia, is rooted in Asian wisdom, and is a bearer of Asian spiritual values and outlooks. Until the twentieth century, Zen existed only in the Far East. Eastern people grasp the universe as a whole in motion and experience themselves as inserted into the flowing stream of the whole, whereas Westerners strive after a goal that defines the meaning of their lives and which is inscribed in the texture of the world that surrounds them and the duties it imposes. The difference between these basic outlooks is apparent. Yesterday, there seemed to be no connection between the two hemispheres. Today, the West has opened itself to the East in a previously unimaginable way, and Zen is playing a great role in this opening. The most extensive and populous of the earth's continents, Asia is neither ethnically, politically, socially, nor even culturally and spiritually a unified whole. The major cultures of India and China are very different from each other, and there are many smaller independent ethnic groups in the giant continent. A special feature of Zen is precisely its close connection to different Asian cultures, between which it builds bridges. Zen does not spring from a single source but was born from the confluence of several Asian traditions.

In the West we tend to summarize the Eastern ways of meditation in a single general concept, whether in appreciation or in admonition. Zen figures prominently in these convenient, generalized images. As a consequence of the West's interest in Zen in this century, there has been a reevaluation of Asian culture. Whereas interest was previously confined to the realm of scholarship, with little attention paid to the authentic core of Asian spiritual experience, today the attention of Westerners is directed to the inner values and spiritual riches of the East. This change has nothing to do with Westerners' curiosity about the exotic but comes from a belatedly understood sense of their own needs and a longing for spiritual fulfillment.

The meditation movement in the West, which has been inspired by the East, must be seen against the background of the spiritual situation of the twentieth century. The triumph of scientific reason brought the development of human power to a peak in the technology and the wars of our time, yet these achievements have also led us into narrow straits. The one-sidedly cerebral development of Western civilization seems the chief culprit in the accumulation of disasters that are often feared to be the prelude to a final catastrophe. The second half of the century has seen a reaction against this. Among the manifold currents that are seen as counterforces or antidotes, Zen is one of the most promising, though in this context Zen has often been seriously deformed by extraneous influences in a complex process extending over several decades and involving various motives.

It is clear from a retrospective study of the history of Zen in Asia that the forces at work in Zen stand in sharp contrast to the one-sidedness of the West. Originating within Buddhism, Zen belongs in its very essence to this Asian religion, whose defining traits it shares. This is particularly true for Zen's relation to reason—to reflective, analytical, and systematic thinking. Professional scholars of religion number Buddhism among the mystical religions, those directed inwards and grounded in ineffable depth-experiences. That has been an essential feature of Buddhism since the days of its founder Shākya-muni, whose enlightenment is regarded by Buddhists of all schools as the pinnacle of human experience, to be imitated in worshipful reverence. Yet despite the primacy of experience and meditation, many highly differentiated philosophical systems have been developed in Buddhism, even within the various branches, so that one may well speak of this religion's ambivalent relation to reason.

In Zen, the meditation school of Mahāyāna Buddhism, experience has an uncontested primacy and is seen as uniquely normative; yet in classical Zen, intellectual elements play a substantial role. The heritage Zen has carried into this century includes not only a wealth of experience but models of thinking that supplement those of Western philosophy. Though the experiential richness is most striking, intellectual values such as the holistic worldview, the awareness of psycho-physical unity, and the consciousness of belonging to the cosmos are inseparably connected with Zen experience. The non-rational experiences proper to Zen can make up for the lacks that have become apparent in Western civilization. The story of how Zen has brought this wisdom of yesterday into the West's rationalistic present is complex and fascinating. Clarifying its phases, we can discern the paths along which an integration of Zen vision and Western reason may proceed.

To understand the recent impact of Zen in the West, a good knowledge of the Zen movement from its beginnings is needed. The Indian roots must not be overlooked. But most important is the placing of Zen as a school of Chinese and Japanese Buddhism, one which early on branched out into several lines. The chief practices underwent many variations of articulation and emphasis. In the web of influences from Eastern spirituality, Zen owes its greatest debts to Indian Yoga and Chinese Taoism. It also had many contacts, both in attraction and in repulsion, with the esoteric movements so prevalent in the wider religious context. A historical survey provides a key to the Zen movement of the twentieth century.

The Western reception of Zen began soon after the turn of the century, when both the cultural world associated with Zen and actual Zen practice began to spread to wider circles. The first initiative came from the East, but the West soon took an active role in appropriating these influences. Several phases can be distinguished in the West's reception of Zen. Progress has been rapid and has not yet stopped. Zen has put down deep roots in Western spiritual life and, unless all indications are misleading, the consequences will be lasting. We must assume that the twentieth century has begun a new era in the history of Zen.

The surprising novelty of the phenomenon should not lead us to neglect the activities of Zen in the Japanese homeland. In Kyoto, the ancient capital, an original Japanese philosophy was produced that strives for a synthesis of Eastern and Western thought. For the first time in its history Zen is coming to reflect on itself. Significant also is the scholarly research on Zen in connection with various disciplines. Archeological finds, translations, and critical assessments of Zen traditions, along with penetrating studies of their content, have led to textual clarifications that now comprise a considerable body of work. For modern psychology the data of Zen not only are an interesting object of research but also promise to enrich therapeutic methods. As the century nears its end, several themes have been lumped together in what is called the New Age movement. This appeals to the Zen experience, which is supposed to create an integral consciousness announcing a new epoch. Finally, the encounter between Christianity and the Eastern religions has been saluted by leading intellectuals as the most important event in this time of upheaval. This is seen and evaluated differently by Buddhists and Christians but is of great significance to both parties. If it succeeds, the Buddhist-Christian encounter can bring into harmony the knowledge proper to each tradition, one supplementing the other without loss of their identities. These are the themes we shall be rehearsing in the following pages.

ZEN
BUDDHISM
IN THE
2 0TH
CENTURY

One

___

ZEN IN
THE WEST

T he beginning of the twentieth century marks a turning point in many fields, and we are now astonished at the depth of the changes that were then inaugurated—notably the way that Far Eastern cultures and religions began to pervade the Western world. This importation can certainly be taken as a sign of the vitality of Asian religions, but in the case of Buddhism, it should also be noted that Western research into Buddhism, launched during the nineteenth century, contributed to the Buddhist revival, notably in Sri Lanka. A similar story could be told for Hinduism. The encounter between Western scientific rationality and Eastern religious wisdom was mutually challenging and beneficial and continues to be so.

The new interreligious situation was dramatically illuminated by the World's Parliament of Religions held during the Exposition in Chicago in 1893. That year, representatives of almost all the world's creeds gathered together for a week in September, and the Asian religions came flamboyantly to the fore. They were no longer the recondite topics of a select circle of scholars but living forces embodied in such remarkable personalities as India's Vivekānanda (1863–1902), founder of the Ramakrishna Mission, and Sri Lanka's Anagarika Dharmapāla (1864–1933), founder of the Buddhist Mahabodhi Society. The spell cast by these men on hundreds of influential listeners marked the arrival of Buddhism and Hinduism in the West. Zen Buddhism, unfortunately, was less forcefully presented by the Rinzai Zen abbot Shaku Sōen (1858–1919), whose English was not adequate to the occasion. A man of international vision who had studied at the progressive Keio University founded by Fukuzawa Yukichi (1835–1901), Shaku Sōen did have some success in his activities behind the scenes. He made friends with the publisher and scholar Paul Carus (1852–1919) and recommended a young disciple of his as an assistant to Carus in the projected translation of a series of Oriental texts. The disciple was Suzuki Daisetsu, better known as Daisetz T. Suzuki (1870–1966). Shaku Sōen thus lit the match that brought about a conflagration of Zen in the West.

Suzuki, who on leaving high school had begun to practice Zen under Imagita Kōsen (1816–92), his master's predecessor as abbot of the historic Rinzai temple Enkakuji in Kamakura, used his new position to acquire a familiarity with Anglo-American culture and a mastery of the English language that stood him in good stead in his great mission of bridging the two hemispheres. His marriage to an American woman who shared his broad religious sympathies gave him deep roots in the West while taking nothing from his fidelity to his Zen background. The American writer of most importance to him was William James (1842–1910), whose influence is palpable in Suzuki's psychologizing style. This affinity with James helped Suzuki find his way into the hearts of his Western listeners. As a Rinzai Buddhist, Suzuki focused on the experience of satori (enlightenment), the quintessence of experience in his view, and on the paradoxical koans that lead to that experience. *Satori* and *koan* were to become the Zen terms most familiar to Western ears, terms to which Suzuki had lent a powerful aura. He neglected the quieter meditative style of the other major Zen school, Sōtō, and its insistence on meditation in everyday life. This neglect is not merely a superficial deficiency; it profoundly affects the character of what has been called "Suzuki Zen," leading to an excessive emphasis on the paradoxical and irrational.

His labors for the implantation of Zen in the West chiefly took a literary form in the first half of his long life. He left the United States in 1908 and went on a world tour. During the following thirty years he devoted himself to the study of Zen, becoming, as he says in an autobiographical sketch, "the first to make a special study of Zen in English."[1] Though he never ventured a systematic presentation of Zen, he was able to cover all its aspects in a prolific output that included such immensely influential works as the three volumes of *Essays in Zen Buddhism*, which first appeared in London from 1927 to 1934 and have been reprinted and translated many times since then. No less popular was the introductory trilogy comprising *An Introduction to Zen Buddhism* (1934), *The Training of the Zen Buddhist Monk* (1934), and *Manual of Zen Buddhism* (1935). Suzuki was no mere regurgitator; he constantly reinterpreted the message he transmitted, adapting it to Western concerns and deliberately highlighting certain key themes. This he did with increasing boldness as his stature not only as a scholar but as a genuine sage was recognized.

Meanwhile, in Germany, Zen had made an entrance under the prestigious auspices of Rudolf Otto, the Marburg philosopher of religion. In 1925 he wrote the preface to the first book on Zen in German, a collection of classical texts translated by a Zen Buddhist layman, Ōhasama Shūei, under the title *Zen—Living Buddhism in Japan*. This preface is still worth reading, as is his later essay, "Numinous Experience in Zazen." In this essay he points out the close association of mysticism with paradox, in Meister Eckhart and Angelus Silesius, for example:

Buddhist nirvana requires a paradoxical negative theology of a special kind, for all positive expressions of it are doomed to collapse. Its absolute otherness to all our concepts becomes most evident in Mahāyāna, especially in its most distinctive school, still flourishing today, the Dhyāna school, which in Japanese is called Zen. Zen, too, occasionally ends in the bizarre and overstrained, in piquant oddities, in *bon mots*, in delight in whatever is curious and unexpected. Yet in its essence it is born from the deepest earnestness of the numinous that transcends reason. At the same time this is carried to such a pitch in Zen that we, who are chiefly preoccupied with the rational aspect of this religion, are at first completely incapable of realizing that this is religion at all, and indeed religion of a quite uncommon strength and depth. Zen is the irrational taken to the extreme and almost torn loose from all rational schemata whatever. If one sees it thus, this entire phenomenon which at first seems completely baffling becomes understandable and can be fitted into place. . . . The solemnity of the numinous, which generally pervades Buddhist ritual and the behavior of the more refined monks, is also to be found in the wonderful temples, halls, religious sculptures, cultic acts and personal attitudes of Zen. . . . The Zen monks are practical mystics, for they connect like Benedict work and prayer, cultivating the land like the Benedictines or devoting themselves according to their talents to higher labors of creative art in painting and sculpture. . . . But all this is not their essential trait. I asked a venerable old abbot in a serene and elegant Zen monastery in Tokyo what the "fundamental idea of Zen" was. Forced into this way of dealing with the questions, he had to come up with some "idea." He said: "We believe that samsāra and nirvana are not different but the same and that each one should find the Buddha-heart in his own heart." But in truth neither is this the principal matter, for this is still "something said," still "doctrine," still tradition. The principal matter of Zen is not a fundamental *idea* but a fundamental *experience*.[2]

Otto goes on to note the total dedication the Zen quest requires, as symbolized in the "monstrous" figure of Bodhidharma sitting in silence for nine years before a wall. This quest is not an introspective burrowing nor an effort at "self-redemption," but a sudden opening of one's "heavenly eye." It yields an ecstatic, ineffable vision of the absolute in the everyday, which cannot be transmitted by words but must be found anew by each person. Otto acknowledged his debt for his precocious appreciation of Zen to essays published by D. T. Suzuki in *The Eastern Buddhist* in 1922, but his own sensitivity to the personalities and the art of Zen remains remarkable. Only a few years earlier, his Munich colleague Friedrich Heiler had missed the encounter with Zen in his book *Buddhist Concentration* (1918), in which Zen is depreciated as a distortion of the meditative technique of earliest Buddhism.

In his old age, D. T. Suzuki added to his literary work a new role as lecturer. World War II marks a caesura in his life. In the post-war period he was the principal spokesman for the epochal breakthrough of Zen in the West, which took place chiefly in the United States. His lecture courses in American universities, especially Columbia University, and his public lectures in many American and European cities (beginning with English and American tours in 1936) had a huge impact. The theme was always Zen, but his concern was less with conveying factual information than with leading people to ultimate truth. His orientation became predominantly philosophical, in contrast to the psychological preoccupations of his earlier writings in which the metaphysical implications of Zen were neglected. But as one of his students once told me, Suzuki's affection for philosophy was that of "a would-be philosopher." In Eckhart's terms, he was more a *Lebemeister* than a *Lesemeister*—more a master of living than of reading.

Suzuki's pioneering work in bringing Zen to the West extends over the greater part of the twentieth century. The degree to which his writings became well-known is attested by the numerous epigones who diluted and sometimes distorted his work beyond recognition. His image of Zen called forth the most various echoes in the West. His achievement in releasing Zen from its maternal Buddhist soil and his penchant for psychologizing and universalizing inevitably tended to obscure the original Buddhist character of Zen. His audience, who had heard again and again from their respected masters that Zen is neither a religion nor a philosophy, were led to interpret Zen in their own way and to associate it with manners of expression foreign to traditional Buddhism. Japanese Zen Buddhists were frequently amazed at the metamorphoses Zen underwent in the West and noted marked differences from the received forms of Japanese Zen. The beatnik or beat movement, which flourished in California in the fifties, was popular with many Zen adherents, and the phrase *beat Zen* came into use, in contrast to *square Zen*. Young people breaking out of the hypertechnological Western consumer society found in Zen mysticism a new lifestyle that gained extra appeal from the fact that this paradoxical Zen seemed to be a slap in the face of convention and rational thought. Esoteric groups latched onto Suzuki, misinterpreting his cognizance of Zen's esoteric elements as an interest in miracles, magic, and parapsychology. Above all, the reception of Suzuki's message was characterized by a hypertrophy of Zen's psychological aspects. Though it undoubtedly opens new perspectives to psychology, as we shall see in a later chapter, it is incorrect to see Zen as a primarily psychological technique. In some places in Japan, psychological techniques were applied with the aim of forcing an experience in a rapid abbreviated course of Zen practice. Such methods, along with hypnosis, psychedelic drugs, and the like, are firmly rejected by the normative masters of the Rinzai and Sōtō schools.

The popularity of Zen naturally brought many Westerners to Japan, a country with a living Zen tradition, and many Japanese masters traveled to America and Europe to meet the demand for authentic instruction. Zen halls appeared in San Francisco in 1928 and in Los Angeles in 1929; in New York, the Buddhist Society of America, later the First Zen Institute for America, was formed in 1931. A great variety of Zen forms was propagated—those of the traditional Buddhist schools and lineages, with variants introduced by individual masters, and also secularized forms, which tended to dissolve the religiously Buddhist character of Zen. Whether Zen was bound to be denatured by this transportation to the West became a serious question. Did the changes amount merely to necessary modernization and inculturation, or did they affect Zen's central core? When Christians began to devote themselves to Zen meditation, these problems of identity were accentuated—a topic we shall examine in depth in a later chapter.

We have seen, then, that the Western reception of Zen inaugurated at the start of the century went far beyond the modifications and transformations of its centuries-long history in Asia. The transition from the Eastern to the Western hemisphere, despite every effort to maintain continuity, inevitably requires new versions of Zen. The pioneering figure of Suzuki is clearly of a different order from the leading Zen masters of previous centuries. Are we in the middle of a breakthrough that is affecting essential elements of the tradition? It is clear at least that the multiform Zen tradition, whose history is so rich in change, has undergone significant enlargements and metamorphoses during the twentieth century.

Two

ZEN PHILOSOPHY AND WESTERN THOUGHT

Though Zen Buddhism cannot be considered a philosophy and though it has never presented itself clothed in philosophical interpretation, the expression "Zen philosophy" arouses no surprise today. In fact there is a considerable body of modern literature devoted to Zen philosophy. A study of Zen in the twentieth century cannot neglect its philosophical aspect.

Over a century ago European scholars argued vehemently about whether or not Buddhism was a philosophy. The question can be considered closed. Despite philosophical elements in all Buddhist schools and philosophical lines of thought in Buddhist teaching, Buddhism is seen today as a world religion, not a philosophy. This is true for all Buddhist schools, including the Zen Buddhist school of Mahāyāna Buddhism.

Nonetheless, especially strong intellectual forces are activated in Zen, the same forces that operate in philosophical thinking. The difference is that in Zen these forces are directed against philosophy as a system. Zen guards itself against all conceptualization and verbalization that proceed from rational thinking. Buddhism, especially Mahāyāna Buddhism, contains philosophical currents and systems, but Zen confronts professional philosophy with a great laugh. During the twentieth century, the radically anti-philosophical character of Zen has attracted many Westerners.

In this very period, a new attitude toward philosophy and its problems established itself within the Zen movement. Philosophical thinking—partly rooted in the Zen tradition and partly stemming from the contemporary philosophical climate—has given a boost to Zen today.

PHILOSOPHICAL ELEMENTS IN THE ZEN TRADITION

In the history of Zen, philosophical motives are prominent in the intellectual background of the movement. Many modern Zen disciples are amazed to find that the early Mahāyāna sutras or the Chinese wisdom books of Lao-tzu and Chuang-tzu expressed ideals that have become familiar to them during their long practice of Zen. However, in the literature of Zen, both Chinese and Japanese, the philosophical content remains unarticulated and there is no reflective explication of the quotations from sutras scattered throughout the texts. Only in the present century has this situation begun to change. Again, this change is due in large part to Suzuki's pioneering work. For a long time his essays on Zen Buddhism were not properly appreciated because of their seemingly unscholarly composition. In many of them he points out the close links between Zen and certain Mahāyāna sutras, especially the *Perfection of Wisdom Sutras*, the *Avatamsaka Sutra*, and the *Lankāvatāra Sutra*. These sutras form the core of the Chinese schools of Buddhism, in which they were elaborately interpreted for several centuries. Zen breaks with the habit of philosophizing on sutra doctrines, but the inspiration that springs from the sutras lives as freshly as a fish in water in the proverbs and the behavior of the

Zen masters, as recorded in the classical koan collections that are the literary high point of the movement. Their indulgence in paradox stems from an excess of insight and testifies to a philosophical capacity in no degree inferior to that of specialists in Buddhist doctrine.

The rich philosophical content of the Mahāyāna sutras is put exclusively at the service of praxis in the Zen writings, with a view to the experience of oneness. Unity and multiplicity, sameness and difference, objectivity and subjectivity, the identity of all reality with the Buddha nature or the true self—these and other philosophically charged themes take shape in an unphilosophical, concrete way. What is intimated in the bizarre wordplay and grotesque gestures of earlier generations is worked through in all its implications in assiduous meditative practice, bringing to light wide-reaching and profound problems for philosophical reflection, such as the mutual implication of all things in the unity of the cosmos, the power of the negation surpassing all differentiation, and the transformation of conscience in the experience of unity. The fact that these themes are presented to the mind in dynamic exercise rather than as objective data increases their appeal.

During the twentieth century the Zen movement in the West has increasingly appropriated Zen's traditional philosophical legacy. A glance at the countless books on Zen that have appeared in quick succession confirms the increasing significance of philosophical approaches since the beginning of the century. Scarcely a single book in a European language contents itself with practical advice and mere description. Philosophical reflection has clearly taken Zen in hand. Suzuki's effort, which he himself frustrated, to keep Zen free of theoretical reflection has failed, and his warnings have fallen on deaf ears.

There has been a marked effort, not only among scholars, to grasp the essence of Zen in such a way as to allow a systematic exposition of its basic principles. This has been the prevailing goal of books on Zen. Meanwhile, historical research has concentrated on the source material, and the valuable translations that have appeared in great number have not, for the most part, been content with a merely philological contribution but have sought through commentary and analysis to penetrate as deeply as possible into the texts and to clarify their philosophical relevance. One should note also the many studies that compare Zen and Western philosophy, whether to show their heterogeneity or their similarities. The mutually challenging encounter with Western thought has brought a new understanding of the Zen movement as one of the great intellectual achievements of human history. The philosophical awareness of its relevance as a worldview, which Zen now enjoys and which is one of the characteristics of twentieth century Zen, has facilitated its spectacular rise to prominence in contemporary culture.

THE DISCOVERY OF DŌGEN AS A THINKER

Zen Master Dōgen (1200–1253) was for a long time principally known as the founder of the Japanese Sōtō school of Zen and as a zealous proponent of zazen (sitting erect in meditation). At the beginning of the twenties, great interest was aroused in the Japanese cultural world by a long essay on the "Monk Dōgen" ("Shamon Dōgen"), which appeared first in reviews, then as a book, by Watsuji Tetsurō, a professor of the then Imperial University of Tokyo. Watsuji, a scholar and respected man of letters, had discovered the intellectual significance of Dōgen, until then little known outside the Sōtō school, and had immersed himself deeply in Dōgen's writings, which had not noticeably influenced Japanese culture during the seven hundred years during which they had been the exclusive property of the school. Watsuji brought Dōgen's work into the public eye. He writes that, though not a member of the Sōtō school, he wanted to show "the true face" of the Zen master to his contemporaries and arouse interest in "an outstanding religious personality" without whom, in his opinion, "the essence of our culture cannot be understood."[1] Countering the objection that it is impossible to understand Dōgen without practicing zazen, Watsuji points out that since the master carefully recorded his thoughts in writing, he was convinced he could share the True Dharma through the written word. Though well aware of the inadequacy of his effort, Watsuji felt compelled to make known the "strong personality" who had impressed him so deeply. He writes:

> I do not entertain any confidence of having understood Dōgen's truth as it really is and I do not assert that my explanation is the only one. But I wish at least to open the way to a new account in which Dōgen will appear no longer as the Dōgen of a single house but as the Dōgen for humanity, no longer as the patriarch of a school but as our Dōgen. I venture to put forward such bold statements since I know that up to now, within the precincts of the sect, Dōgen has been killed.[2]

Watsuji is sharply critical of the Sōtō school of his day for failing to bring to light the profound insights of its founder's writings. The biographies to date revealed no real familiarity with Dōgen's work, Watsuji felt. Hence it was his duty as a cultural historian to share his knowledge, albeit partial, of the great philosopher he recognized in the old Zen master.

Note the expressions "Dōgen for humanity" and "our Dōgen." These phrases indicate precisely the two basic traits that have been brought out in subsequent Dōgen studies, namely, the modernity and universality of the Zen master. "Our Dōgen" has something to say to us today. After seven hundred years he is modern again, and his significance is not confined to the Sōtō school. By reason of his modernity and universality he reaches beyond spatial and temporal frontiers, and like Zen he is known and studied outside the East as timeless.

Watsuji's essay aroused a strong response in Japan, and the philosopher of the Kyoto school, Tanabe Hajime (1885–1962), another major figure in the cultural life of Japan in the first half of the century, expressed his full agreement in a long essay, "A Personal View of the Philosophy of the *Shōbōgenzō*."[3] He shared Watsuji's high esteem for Dōgen and expressly thanked Watsuji in his foreword for discovering this "outstanding metaphysician and precursor of Japanese philosophy." Tanabe lavished praise on the "depth and exactness of Dōgen's thought" and stressed his modernity. Dōgen, he felt, pointed the way to "the systematic thinking of contemporary philosophy." However, Tanabe's personal interpretation of the *Shōbōgenzō* was of only slight help for a correct understanding of that difficult text.

Tanabe's essay can be seen as a continuation of Watsuji's persuasive call. Inwardly moved by the spiritual depth of Dōgen's religious thought, the two men inaugurated a new age of Dōgen studies in Japan. The first systematic presentation of Dōgen's work in Japanese, still unsurpassed today, came from Akiyama Hanji, who was neither a Sōtō monk nor a man of letters but spent his long life as teacher and headmaster of a provincial high school. He modestly titled the result of his years of strenuous, patient research *Studies in*

Dōgen (1935).[4] His book is distinguished by clarity of style and orderly exposition. A comparable total presentation was produced exactly forty years later (1975) in English by Professor Hee-Jin Kim, currently teaching in the United States.[5] Besides these two general presentations there exist as yet only a number of monographs and more or less carefully annotated textual translations. Akiyama, inspired by Watsuji, thanked Tanabe in his foreword for help in the publication of his book. He concentrates on the philosophical content of Dōgen's writing and stresses especially its ontological aspect but also deals with the principles of Zen praxis proper to Dōgen, namely, the unity of practice and enlightenment and the unique import of zazen.

In the pre-war years Dōgen was already a subject of discussion in Japanese academic circles, thanks to the pioneers Watsuji, Tanabe, and Akiyama. His name was also mentioned more and more frequently at the yearly congresses of scholars of religion. It is not surprising, then, that the alarmed Sōtō school joined in. The book *Zen Master Dōgen as the Founder of a School*, composed by a professor of Komazawa University, a Sōtō institution, reclaims Dōgen for the Sōtō school, which considers him its founder.[6] After the war, there was an increase in publications on Dōgen as well as new editions of his works; this continues undiminished today under the leadership of the professors of Komazawa University.

Masunaga Reihō (1902–81) of the Sōtō school deserves special mention, for he has sought more than any of his colleagues to show Dōgen's modernity and his eminent significance for the West. He wished to do for Dōgen's Zen what Suzuki had done for the Rinzai school, but his efforts were unfortunately terminated by severe illness and a premature death. How much the realization of his project meant to him can be seen from his lament: "The knowledge of Zen in the West only rarely extends to the numerous Zen sects of Sōtō"

(1958).[7] Soon, however, this remark no longer applied. The extensive chapter on Dōgen in my 1959 book, *Zen—Geschichte und Gestalt*, one of the earliest Western assessments of Dōgen, owes much to Masunaga's friendship and assistance and to the hours spent under his guidance, in a circle of interested friends, working through chapters from the *Shōbōgenzō*. My 1961 essay on the religious metaphysics of Dōgen clarifies the central point of Dōgen's thought, his ontological view of the Buddha-nature.[8] The same theme is treated by Abe Masao, a representative of the Kyoto school, in his English study, "Dōgen on Buddha Nature."[9] The Dōgen literature of the last three decades, containing many treatments of individual topics and explanations of his texts, is extremely rich. There are several complete translations of his chief work, the *Shōbōgenzō*, in European languages, which are certainly useful even if not completely satisfying.

The modernity of Dōgen's work is probably the key to the revival of interest in him in this century. Several books of the *Shōbōgenzō* deal with perennial human questions, still pressing today: life and death, being and not-being, being and time. The central, comprehensive chapter on the Buddha-nature culminates in a series of statements on the being of the Buddha-nature, the nothingness of the Buddha-nature, and the impermanence of the Buddha-nature—purely metaphysical utterances in which ontological realism, negation, and becoming are brought into accord. These problems are treated not just theoretically but in an earnestly religious way; that is, the theory is constantly anchored in and referred to meditative practice. Indeed, enlightenment is identified with practice: it is by sitting in zazen that one manifests one's enlightenment.

Another modern feature of Dōgen is the original language he created, an achievement that appeals to twentieth century philosophers, who accord such great importance to language. The Korean scholar Kim pays particular attention to Dōgen's power of expression, noting, "To Dōgen life is an incessant round of hermeneutical activities" that he was able to express in creative, original terms.[10] Thomas P. Kasulis, a young American Zen researcher, has published an essay interpreting the work of the "incomparable philosopher" from a hermeneutical viewpoint.[11] He praises not only the "richness of language" of the "masterpiece" of the "profound thinker" but urges, for real understanding, attention to the "intimate presence of Dōgen himself" in his writings. Only through intimate association with the master, in which the reader and the author actively cooperate, is correct reading possible. Kasulis points especially to two chapters of the *Shōbōgenzō*, "Kattō" ("Entanglements") and "Mitsugo" (literally, "Secret Word"). The expression *mitsugo* can be understood in an esoteric sense; Dōgen interprets it as intimate communication.[12] Intensive reading forges a union of reader and author. The clarification and interpretation of Dōgen's work presents modern philosophers of language with a rewarding task.

From these hermeneutical premises it follows that the reader's understanding of Dōgen never remains the same but undergoes alteration in the course of a longer, intensive involvement with the master's writings. Thus when his thinking is compared once again with Western philosophy, there are new and surprising consequences. A considerable literature is concerned with the theme "Dōgen and Heidegger." Other philosophers, too, such as Hegel, Schelling, Kierkegaard, Sartre, Whitehead, and even the Indian thinker Shankara are placed in connection with Dōgen. The comparisons are not always happy ones and have produced only scanty results. But they clearly indicate that Dōgen transcends himself in his writings. Just this marks his thought as creative and universal. The work of

Dōgen, in which the philosophical element comes strongly to the fore, has a major role to play in clarifying the importance of Zen for twentieth century culture. Since Watsuji's discovery, Dōgen studies have remained vital, first in Japan, then in the West, without any sign of exhaustion; on the contrary, it is increasingly clear that this Zen master and his work have not yet completely and definitively been given their place in the cosmos of human thought.

THE KYOTO SCHOOL

The Kyoto School has won a place in the history of Japanese philosophy and in the history of Zen Buddhism. The school, though considered representative of Zen philosophy, did not arise in the immediate environment of a Zen school, for example in a monastery or in a university connected with a Zen school. Instead, it was founded and nurtured by experienced Zen philosophers whose task was not the exposition of Zen Buddhist thinking in a philosophical system but the penetration of European philosophy by the spirit of Zen. Thus arose that unique synthesis of Eastern and Western thought that has given the Kyoto school a special significance.[13]

Nishida Kitarō The founder of the school, Nishida Kitarō (1870–1945), was anchored in Zen, his spiritual home.[14] In youth, as his diaries show, he dedicated himself to Zen practice and attained Zen enlightenment. Like D. T. Suzuki he was of provincial origin. After studying at Tokyo University he eked out a modest existence in the country as a middle and high school teacher, then taught German and philosophy for a short period at the Peers' School (Gakushuin) in Tokyo (1909). At the age of forty he was called to the Imperial

University, to whose fame he lent new luster. In the second year of his teaching he published his ground-breaking book *An Inquiry into the Good* (1911),[15] the best known and most widely read of his many writings. In his lectures he dealt with Western philosophy, at first immersing himself in the phenomenological and descriptive orientations of Brentano, Husserl, Bergson, and James, popular at the time, and later chiefly with German philosophy from Kant through Fichte and Hegel, Neo-Kantianism, and Dilthey to Heidegger. He paid particular attention to the mystics Pseudo-Dionysius, Eckhart, Nicholas of Cusa, and Boehme. These currents from the West enriched him intellectually, but he did not succumb to Western modes of thought.

In his maiden work on the good he avoided Zen expressions, but the "pure experience" that he described and sought to provide the ground for is the experience of Zen enlightenment. D. T. Suzuki, Nishida's friend since youth, wrote in a text "How Nishida is to be Read," later printed as an introduction to *An Inquiry into the Good*: "In my view Nishida's philosophy of absolute nothingness or his logic of the self-identity of absolute contradictories is difficult to understand if one is not sufficiently acquainted with the Zen experience."[16] Suzuki knew his friend's heartfelt aspiration to bring together Western philosophy and Buddhist thinking. He directed Nishida to William James's description of religious experience. In later years, Suzuki was full of admiration for the intellectual power of his companion in thought and received much from him. The two were united by their common goal of forging an entry and building esteem for Far Eastern—more precisely, Zen—thought in the West.

Nishida's early philosophy of pure experience drew from the source of Zen, which is in its essence experience. Later the Zen element came out more clearly. From Nishida's transitional period

21

came *Intuition and Reflection in Self-Consciousness* (1917), *Art and Morality* (1923), and *From the Acting to the Seeing* (1927); in his mature major work *Fundamental Problems of Philosophy* (1933), but already in his essay on "The Self-Identity of Absolute Contradictories" (1930), Nishida found his definitive standpoint, the logic of the place of nothingness, which leads to the religious problem discussed in his last writings, "Towards a Philosophy of Religion with the Concept of Pre-Established Harmony as Guide" (1944) and "The Logic of the Place of Nothingness and the Religious Worldview" (1945).[17—22]

In these two late essays the prevalent modes of his thought are brought together, and Zen inspiration is evident in both the progress of the argument and the texts quoted. In the first of these essays Nishida takes thoughts from Leibniz, Nicholas of Cusa, and Spinoza and tries to reformulate them from the standpoint of his "logic of place." With Leibniz, he affirms the meaningful unity of the real but remarks critically that pre-established harmony cannot be "the logical principle of the structure of the historical world" in which contradictoriness prevails. This principle is rather "the self-identity of contradictions." It is on this principle that moral activity is founded. The self-identity of contradictories is "the root of man's religious exigency" and has its goal in "absolute negation" in which "there is nothing which can be negated."[23] In the argument of the essay, the metaphysics of Mahāyāna Buddhism is normative. Nishida refers to the *Perfection of Wisdom Sutras* and to the philosophical *The Awakening of Faith in Mahāyāna* (Sanskrit: *Mahāyāna Sraddhotpāda Sāstra*; Japanese: *Daijō Kishinron*). He is vividly aware of the principle of the mutual unimpeded interpenetration of phenomena, a core teaching of the *Avatamsaka Sutras*. He quotes sayings of Chinese and Japanese Zen masters, especially Lin-chi (Japanese: Rinzai) and Dōgen, the heads of the two leading schools. Two short utterances from the collected sayings of the Chinese master (*Rinzairoku*) indicate the freedom of the enlightened one: "He is master of himself wherever he goes," and "As he stands all is right with him."[24]

The high point of the book *Genjōkōan* in the *Shōbōgenzō* is Dōgen's famous saying about the self: ". . . to study the way of Buddha is to study the self, and to study the self is to forget the self; to forget the self is to be enlightened by all things [Dharmas]."[25] Nishida quotes this in both late essays as expressing the necessity of self-negation in order to be a true self:

> In the depths of the self there is that which transcends the self. And yet it is not something external to the self, something merely other than the self. There is the dimension of existential contradiction, about which we are always going astray. Religious faith involves precisely this dimension wherein the self discovers itself as a bottomlessly contradictory entity. Subjectively, this discovery takes the form of "realizing peace of mind," and objectively, of "experiencing salvation."[26]

Such passages are typical of the existential gravity of "The Logic of the Place of Nothingness and the Religious Worldview," composed as a testament for his disciples in the last year of his life, during the terror of the air raids in the closing months of the war. The essay might be seen as the Japanese counterpart to certain pages of Kierkegaard's journals.

Underlying the dizzying dialectics one perceives an impassioned religious tone:

> We know of our eternal death. This is our existential condition. At the same time, we already exist in eternal life. Religious faith entails that the self realize its own contradictory identity of eternal death and eternal life; that is

23

what is involved in religious conversion. Since this is impossible from the standpoint of the objectified self, we
must speak here of the power, the working of God: faith
is the self-determination of the absolute itself. Faith is
grace bestowed. It is God's own voice in the depths of the
self.[27]

In focusing on what lies at the foundation of our self, Nishida
indicates that Zen thought is the center of gravity of this final
summary of his religious ideas, though enhanced by Pure Land and
Christian motifs. (Pure Land Buddhism, based on a set of Indian
sutras, spread from China to Japan, where its most influential propa-
gators were Honen [1133–1212] and Shinran [1173–1262]. Through
faith in Amida [Amitābha] Buddha and the invocation of his name
[*Namu-amida-butsu*], one is assured of rebirth in Amida's Pure Land.)
Nishida distinguishes between the superficial self and the ground of
the self. His language avoids objectifying presentations of God while
making it clear that his philosophy is neither atheistic nor pantheis-
tic. "God appears to the religious self as an event of one's own soul.
It is not a matter of God being conceivable or not conceivable in
merely intellectual terms. What can be conceived or not conceived is
not God."[28] In seeking the logic of the religious event, Nishida
becomes the first Buddhist, as far as I know, to introduce the notion
of the kenosis or self-emptying of God, which has since become a
nodal point of discussion in the dialogue with Western thought:

I hold that when we express God, or the absolute, in logical
terms we must speak in this way. Because God, or the
absolute, stands to itself in the form of a contradictory
entity—namely as its own absolute self-negation. . . . Because it is absolute nothingness, it is absolute being. It is
because of this that we can speak of the divine omniscience
and omnipotence. . . . The true absolute exists in that it

24

returns to itself in the form of the relative. The true absolute One expresses itself in the form of the infinite many. God exists in this world through self-negation. . . . A God merely transcendent and self-sufficient would not be a true God. God must always, in St. Paul's words, empty himself.[29]

He also writes with understanding of the "personalistic" outlook of Christianity, again building the way to a future dialogue.[30]

Nishida created his own mode of thought and world of ideas as he reflected on his experience. Zen is the point of departure and the support of his philosophizing, and Zen themes guide his thought. Even in his lifetime people began to refer to a Nishida school that was opening a new, original way. Enriched and extended by his highly gifted students, this school is now called the Kyoto school.

Tanabe Hajime The second representative of the Kyoto school, Tanabe Hajime (1885–1962), enriched the school's discourse with a strong new line of thought.[31] Born in Tokyo, he studied natural philosophy and mathematics at the Imperial University and continued his studies as a lecturer at Sendai University (1913), publishing several more works on these subjects. At the age of thirty-four he was called to Kyoto University, where he enjoyed an intellectually enriching association with Nishida, who shared his interest in the relationship between the natural and the human sciences.

During his first years in Kyoto, Tanabe was chiefly occupied with European philosophy. Between 1922 and 1924 he studied in Berlin and Leipzig and then went to Freiburg, where he worked with Husserl and became acquainted with Heidegger. On his return to Japan he completed his doctoral dissertation on the philosophy of mathematics, which was the high point of his research in the natural sciences. His philosophical development in the following years pro-

25

ceeded from Husserl's phenomenology to the Hegelian dialectic, which inspired the "dialectic of absolute mediation" that shaped his own thought. In these years he developed his "logic of species,"[32] which he set in critical opposition to Nishida's "logic of place." In the historic former capital his philosophy increasingly manifested a Buddhist hue. When Nishida retired from teaching in 1928, Tanabe succeeded him on the philosophy faculty of Kyoto University.

The end of the war (1945) marks a turning point in Tanabe's intellectual career. During the last war years the philosopher had suffered intensely with the people and had sensed that the conditions of the time called for a new philosophy. He carried out a radical turnaround in his philosophy of metanoetics or penitence, in which religious motives came strongly to the fore. This "nonphilosophical philosophy," as he says in his preface, "maintains the purpose of functioning as a reflection on what is ultimate and as a radical self-awareness, which are the goals proper to philosophy." He could not undertake this philosophy from his own power (*jiriki*). "It is rather a philosophy to be practiced by Other-power (*tariki*), which has turned me in a completely new direction through metanoesis, and has helped me to make a fresh start from the realization of my utter helplessness." Metanoesis signifies, in the first place, remorse for guilt incurred, accompanied by shame and grief; Tanabe addresses its ethical aspect with reference to his own experience. But this metanoesis impels him to a new step, namely, to a philosophy of metanoetics that he calls "the philosophy of Other-power," born of his own deep experience of conversion and resurrection. The new life that has passed through death and resurrection is "granted to me from the transcendent realm of the absolute which is neither life nor death. Since this absolute is the negation and transformation—that is, conversion—of everything relative, it may be defined as absolute nothingness. I experience this absolute nothingness through which I am reborn to new life as nothingness-*qua*-love."[33]

The turnabout of his philosophy of metanoetics brought Tanabe onto the path of Shinran (1173–1262), the major thinker associated with Pure Land faith in Other-power. Tanabe had encountered him previously, but Shinran's experience now appeared in a new light, as parallel to his own. He was now convinced that he had a new and quite independent philosophy to offer. Paradoxically, "once I had arrived at belief in Other-power, I found myself still closer to the spirit of Zen, whose emphasis on self-power is generally considered opposed to Pure Land doctrine." His reflection on his inner rapport with the two contrasting Buddhist schools reveals a symbiosis of polar opposites typical of Buddhist thought and piety. Tanabe writes: "My innate attraction for the idealistic doctrine of self-power made me more sympathetic to the Zen sect than to sects that taught 'salvation by Other-power.' Although I had never undergone discipline in a Zen monastery, I had long been familiar with the discourses of Chinese and Japanese Zen masters. I was ashamed that I still remained an outsider to Zen and could not enter into the depths of its holy truth, and yet I felt closer to Zen than to Shin doctrine."[34]

The religious posture of Tanabe was further complicated by his inclination to Christianity, also expressed in his work *Philosophy as Metanoetics*. As Heisig notes in his preface,

> Tanabe abstained stoically from association with any one religious tradition, Eastern or Western, in order that he might the better address the problem of religion in a more general sense. Some of his commentators judge him closer to Christianity, others to Shin Buddhism, still others to Zen. The evidence to support any of these conclusions is there in abundance, but only because it was his goal to

keep equidistant from all three, thereby to work a general dialectical synthesis of the philosophic core of Zen Buddhism (concern with totality), Nembutsu Buddhism (concern with the individual), and Christianity (concern with species [=concrete history]).[35]

In Takeuchi's opinion, Tanabe's standpoint of absolute criticism permitted him to leap from one philosophical position to another: "Tanabe's pilgrimage in the philosophy of religion, which looks in one sense to have been an aimless wandering from Dōgen to Shinran, from Shinran to Jesus, and then back again to Zen, was actually a consistently rigorous and highly disciplined spiritual journey. . . . Tanabe struggled to sustain a sort of 'philosophical faith' created from philosophy but transcending philosophy."[36]

Some passages in *Philosophy as Metanoetics* illustrate Tanabe's understanding of Zen, which was an unusual one for the Kyoto school. His own lack of a personal experience of enlightenment was not an impediment to his admiration of Zen, though his insistence on counting himself among the ignorant ironically throws into prominence Zen's elitist character. The religion of "ordinary, ignorant persons like me" is faith in Amida.[37] In his view Zen lacks an ethical dimension, a failure he sees as affecting Buddhism in general. Zen, he claims, finds itself constantly in danger of expressing the self-identity of reality in a dialectically unbroken way and "getting stuck in the merely subjective and immanent," because of "a tendency to unite the absolute with the relative on the basis of the principle of self-identity."[38] He warns repeatedly against this danger, to which the majority of Zen practitioners who have not undergone the "Great Death" in intensive koan practice are exposed.

Tanabe's inclination to Christianity reached its apex in the postwar years, when he dealt with Christian philosophy and theology in his books *Existence, Love, and Praxis* (1947) and *Dialectic of Christianity* (1948). In the preface to the latter he describes himself as "one who is becoming a Christian." During this period the basic Buddhist concepts retained their validity, but Tanabe sought to link them with Christian ideas: death and resurrection, nothingness-*qua*-love. This rapprochement with Christianity was, however, short-lived.

In two texts of his final years, "Memento Mori" (1958) and "Dialectic of Death" (1959), he assembled Eastern and Western components for a philosophy of death.[39] In the former text he writes: "If what one must call the philosophy of death is a task imposed on humanity for the present and the future, then in my opinion there is no more powerful approach to it than Zen Buddhist enlightenment."[40] In the middle of the essay he places a koan from the classical collection *Hekiganroku*. In the presence of a dead man a master is asked if human existence is life or death; the master replies: "Neither life nor death." This utterance, the summation of Zen Buddhist wisdom, corresponds to the standpoint of of the Mahāyāna metaphysics, according to which life and death are inseparably one, the front and the back, mutually interpenetrating. "The truth of Zen, which is also the content of the philosophy of death, is in brief the renunciation of satisfying or actuating the self even in its ambition to attain truth and the decision never to be content with a life that is lived immediately, that is, without the reverse side of death, without attention to the menace of death."[41] Tanabe finds in the Christian *memento mori* some connecting thread with the Zen Buddhist attitude, but it is the Mahāyānist dialectic of death that determines his thoughts on the philosophy of death. He remains anchored in the Buddhist traditions of the East.

Nishida and Tanabe are regarded as the founding fathers of the Kyoto school; they are not related as master and disciple. Tanabe,

who belongs "to the ranks of the most original and influential thinkers of modern Japan,"[42] did not merely continue Nishida's inspiring
work but blazed unique paths that increasingly brought them into
conflict, a tension that became almost hostile in the end.[43] This makes
it impossible to fit Tanabe into a "Nishida school." Yet the two
thinkers have a great deal in common, which is why their dialogue
gave rise to a school of thinking in which the common and the
divergent could coexist. The basic intention of the Kyoto school is
evidently the encounter between genuine Japanese thinking and
European intellectuality, an encounter which has produced a variety
of rich rewards. From its beginning the Kyoto school has been
complex, preserving its unity in plurality, its common conviction in
oppositions.

D. T. Suzuki as Philosopher   We have met Suzuki as the best-
known proponent of contemporary Zen Buddhism in the West.
Though he was not a professional philosopher, there are two reasons
for counting him a member of the Kyoto school. First, he was a
member of the Buddhist scholarly circle centered at the university in
Kyoto and was also active in its spiritual milieu. Linked with Nishida
Kitarō by close ties of friendship, he shared his desire to introduce
the West to Oriental spiritual heritage in the form of Zen Buddhism.
Nishida, "the first Japanese person that could be said to have had his
own philosophy," welcomed the intellectual stimulation of his friend.
While he devoted his energies to theoretical philosophy, developing
a logic that, unlike that of the West, was based on personal experience, Suzuki's task was to embody the spirit of Zen, living to the
full the Zen life. In the judgment of an important Japanese scholar
of the early generation, still living, "it can be said that with Suzuki,
Nishida, and Tanabe, Japanese philosophy genuinely became Jap-

anese philosophy." "Nishida initiated this new philosophy and provided a foundation for it . . . his philosophy must be recognized as an epoch in our history of thought."[44]

Suzuki's actualization of the living spirit of Zen is attested in many of his philosophical writings. His capacity to absorb sources was both comprehensive and original and was allied with a skillful discernment in transmitting their contents. We have dealt in the first part of this chapter with the philosophical riches of the Zen heritage, grounded in Mahāyāna sources. Besides producing popular writings, Suzuki devoted himself to lifelong scholarship, studying the Mahāyāna sutras and Chinese Zen literature. As a young man he published a book on the essential traits of Mahāyāna Buddhism. His translation and studies of the *Lankāvatāra Sutra* won the recognition and acclaim of contemporary Buddhologists. His mastery of Mahāyāna terminology is amply demonstrated in his two lectures on "The Essence of Buddhism," delivered before the emperor shortly after the end of the war (1947), in which almost all the central philosophical motifs of Mahāyāna are set forth in concentrated form.[45]

In his work on the Chinese Zen masters, Suzuki's intellectual depth is most apparent in his brief notes and longer commentaries on the patriarch Lin-chi (Japanese: Rinzai), whom he deeply revered. Himself an adherent of the Rinzai school, he regarded its founder as the embodiment of the highest enlightened wisdom. A Japanese monograph titled *The Basic Ideas of Rinzai* shows his deep penetration of the thought of the great Chinese monk.[46] The slender volume *The Zen Doctrine of No-Mind* offers the quintessence of this work in English.[47] His explanation of the famous passage on "the common man of no rank" in the collected sayings of Rinzai assures him a place among those who have really grasped the Zen mind. In a symposium on Zen and psychoanalysis, Suzuki consciously broke through the

31

psychological framework to Zen's philosophical dimension.[48] Research on his Japanese writings, still in its initial stages, should bring the philosophical and scholarly significance of his work into clearer relief.

Though not strictly a member of the Kyoto school, Suzuki's place in this chapter is easy to justify. His restless activity in spreading Zen in the West has often been noted without sufficient attention to his chief contribution, the intellectual transmission of Far Eastern wisdom. His leading role in world culture in this century makes it doubly regrettable that his multi-faceted lifework has not yet been gathered in a complete edition and studied bibliographically and in terms of its influence. An objective assessment, which would of course have to note weaknesses and one-sidedness, is indispensable for the correct assessment of his achievement. However one judges his various insights and utterances, his attractions and repulsions, his literary masterpieces and less-inspired writings, Suzuki stands in the first rank of the cultural bridge builders between Asia and the West during the twentieth century.

Hisamatsu Shin'ichi Among the many pupils of Nishida, Hisamatsu Shin'ichi (1889–1980) and Nishitani Keiji (1900–1990) stand out. Hisamatsu united a university career with the life of a cloistered monk.[49] After his studies at Kyoto University under Nishida, whom he revered all his life as his teacher and Dharma-master, he entered the famous Rinzai monastery Myōshinji and successfully completed the Zen training, without interrupting his scholarly research. He taught at various universities and after Tanabe's retirement occupied the chair in philosophy of religion and Buddhism at Kyoto University from 1943 to 1949. In the following years he gave university courses and lectured in America, Europe, Iran, and India. A circle of students gathered about him in Kyoto and, as a practicing Zen master, he shared with them his understanding of Zen and introduced them to meditation.

Philosophically, his standpoint, as first articulated in his Japanese publications, is characterized by the rejection of every form of theism. An early text on the Far Eastern notion of nothingness, *Tōyōteki Mu no Seikaku* (1939)—translated into German under the author's supervision as *Die Fülle des Nichts* (1975)—attempts to "grasp in words what was beheld immediately in the deep experience of nothingness" in his enlightenment experience, pitting itself against "the unmasterable threat to which every conceptual explication of this nothingness is exposed." Working from personal experience, Hisamatsu gives a concentrated sketch of the essence of nothingness, "the marrow of Buddhism and the essential core of Zen," which is identical with "the self-awakening in me, in which my religious life and my philosophical thinking are rooted." Surveying the various attempts to expound nothingness in conceptual terms, he lists five erroneous ways of understanding nothingness—namely, nothingness as the negation of existence, as the negation of statements, as an idea, as fantasy, and as unconscious. These phenomena differ "clearly and unambiguously from Zen Buddhist nothingness." He explicitly rejects nothingness as a negative statement about God, that is, the so-called *theologia negativa*. The concept of God, he maintains, excludes all definitions of God, even negative ones. Yet he sees strong similarities between these erroneous definitions of nothingness and Zen Buddhist nothingness, and these further impede the adequate comprehension of the experience of nothingness, impossible in any case.[50]

Buri points out "inner tensions and questionable features that cannot be overlooked" and remarks, surprisingly, that "there is a clear parallel between the Catholic doctrine of analogy and Hisamatsu's recurrent characterization of the relation between the concepts of nothingness and what Zen means by nothingness in terms of a notion of similarity which by reason of its dissimilarity points beyond itself."[51] We can hardly suppose that Hisamatsu was influenced by the famous passage on analogy of the Fourth Lateran Council or the vast literature on the concept of God and the *analogia entis*. Had he reflected on the relationship between the *analogia entis* and his own analogies of nothingness, he might have avoided the grave defects in his grasp of "medieval theism"[52] and "medieval theonomy."[53]

In the second half of his treatise, Hisamatsu deals with the characteristics of Zen Buddhist nothingness on the basis of his experience. "Zen nothingness does not present an empty object-free space outside my person, but is my own state of nothingness, namely my self that is 'nothing,'" and this experiential nature of nothingness is linked with "its character of complete indeterminacy." Nothingness is a "not-anything" and is thus brought into the vicinity of emptiness. Hisamatsu, following a Chinese Zen text, enumerates ten meanings of emptiness and notes that "all these marks of emptiness are proper to Zen nothingness in the same way." Nothingness is identical with the self and with the mind (Sanskrit: *citta*): ". . . the 'mind,' namely Zen nothingness," corresponds to the meanings of emptiness and is "unemptily empty." Yet despite the "great similarity between the nothingness of Zen and emptiness," the two are not identical, as is clear from the identity of nothingness with the mind: ". . . the notion of mind cannot be exhaustively compared with emptiness or infinite space." While emptiness possesses no mind and nothing that can be called life, the nothingness of Zen is not lifeless but entirely vital; it has mind and is conscious of itself. Hisamatsu's explanations aim to show the identity of Zen nothingness with the mind or the nature of the mind and the self, an identity experienced in the moment of awakening to the true self. The awakened one enjoys a free, untrammeled mind along with creative energy. Zen nothingness is the mind that produces everything and the true self of the free person who clings to nothing.[54]

The little book we have just summarized offers an early synopsis of Hisamatsu's Zen philosophy as it emerged from reflection on his experience. The main themes are set forth in this text, and the essay "Satori (Self-Awakening)" offers further indications. Self-awakening is the medium and the goal of Zen experience; it lays the foundation for what Hisamatsu considers the only human mode of being that is appropriate to the religion of the postmodern age. He discusses four "images of the human" or "human modes of being," namely, the humanistic, the nihilistic, the theistic, and that based on self-awakening. Self-awakening is the same as the enlightenment experience of Zen and as such is ineffable and inexplicable. Only "the self-expression of awakening" can serve as an account of it. Erroneous manners of expression must be weeded out. "Self-awakening is neither a belief in selfhood nor an objective experience of selfhood; neither is it the desire for selfhood, nor an inner vision of it, nor a knowledge about it; but rather an awakening of selfhood to selfhood itself." Put positively, it is "a fundamental self-awakening of deep dimension which has overcome absolute negation. It is the true self, the true person. Just this self-awakening is the 'Buddha' in Buddhism." Hisamatsu claims the greatest timeliness for the image of the human yielded by self-awakening. It avoids the disadvantages of nihilism and of theism without falling into the "fateful paralysis of modern humanism." Through "the absolute autonomy of the mode of being of self-awakening," one escapes the quandaries of modernity and enters the post-modern epoch.[55]

The essay "Atheism," one of Hisamatsu's last works, translated into German by the Japanese Protestant theologian Takizawa Katsumi, was discussed at a scholarly colloquium at the Mission Academy of Hamburg University in January 1978. In this essay Hisamatsu declares himself an atheist and presents atheism as inevitably entailed by the radical autonomy of the Zen experience of self. Proceeding from Fichte and Kant, he defines religion as "human action according to an autonomous law." "The modern age has developed in such wise that human beings increasingly free themselves from the law of God and submit to their own law." The Zen experience of self corresponds, in his view, to the modern world, which "in its authentic sense is the age of atheism." Nonetheless, although we are radical atheists, we should not "become stuck in modern autonomy. . . . We must remain atheists and at the same time become religious but non-theistic people." To clarify this paradox he introduces the dialectical notion of "autonomous heteronomy," that is, "a heteronomy which includes autonomy in itself." Autonomous heteronomy does not entail dependence. Self-awakening "must be a happening that breaks forth from the self's own ground." The ground here is the I-Self or Wholly Self. Awakening, also called "resurrection," proceeds from "one's own original core of being."

As illustrations, Hisamatsu offers two similes. He compares the renewal or resurrection in awakening with the transformation of the caterpillar into the butterfly, in which "the caterpillar, negating itself, makes itself free from itself and becomes a butterfly." In this process "various external or auxiliary means are operative, but they are not what is proper to the Buddha but mere auxiliaries." What appears to be an outside agency, an Other, is an operation of the Buddha. "But the true, original Buddha who exerts this activity cannot be anything heteronomous or Wholly Other, but must be an autonomous Wholly Self." "The transformation from caterpillar to butterfly must happen autonomously through and through." The cooperation of the chick with the hen in a "simultaneous pushing from within and pecking from without" is popular in Zen literature as an illustration for the assistance of the master in the practitioner's breakthrough to enlightenment. Hisamatsu emphasizes that it is not the pecking from without but the pushing from within that is decisive. "The chicken emerges as such with its own quite independent being in that it breaks the shell from within. Thus there is an original selfhood in the chicken, so that the hen is merely an aid to the realization of the being of the chicken as such. The chicken comes out quite autonomously." Butterfly and chicken exemplify the autonomous, completely independent and free mode of being of the awakened one, identical with the mode of being of the Buddha. "The Buddha who shines through all hindrances never exists outside the I-Self . . . and is then first Buddha when he is this I-Self." "The Buddha who is called the True Buddha is never anything theistic but, as said above, nothing other than the human being who has freed himself from his original crisis. The Buddha exists not as some heteronomous transcendent or immanent something separated from this I-Self, but as something which is strictly identical with this I-Self. True reality is identical with all appearances; its presence is Wholly Self and Buddha, neither immanent nor transcendent."[56]

Hisamatsu's philosophy goes far beyond mere reflection on the Zen experience. In the style of the Kyoto school, it takes Zen nothingness as a point of departure and makes much use of Western modes of thought. Its account of the Zen experience provides one possible interpretation among many—one that invites further discussion and whose uncommon sharpness derives in large part from the heavy use of Western terminology.

Takeuchi Yoshinori Tanabe's principal disciple, Takeuchi Yoshinori (b. 1913), reveals the complexity of the Kyoto school. Faithful to his master, whose work he has tirelessly interpreted and whose *Philosophy as Metanoetics* he has translated impeccably, Takeuchi is at the same time the foremost connoisseur and admirer of the Nishida philosophy, which he has elucidated to Western scholars in many essays and articles. His is a distinctive combination of philosophical acumen and a religiously attuned, harmonious character.

Takeuchi belongs to the Jōdo Shinsū school, in which he enjoys high esteem as the head of a temple. Linked to the Kyoto school by his study and teaching at Kyoto University (1964–76) and through his teacher Tanabe, his literary work places him in the front rank of the school's philosophers. More than anyone else, he has made its intellectual heritage accessible to wide circles in numerous studies, precise commentaries, and outstanding translations.

Takeuchi's contribution to the dialogue with Western thought, especially with Christianity, has been facilitated by the wealth and solidity of his knowledge and his human qualities of openness and benevolence. His combination of Zen philosophy and reverence for Amida has been for many Westerners a surprising revelation of the breadth of the Buddhist religion. His excellent book on early Buddhism, which opens new perspectives, originated from a series of lectures he gave as a guest at the University of Marburg.[57] Interpreters of this kind can greatly assist the dialogue of the world religions at this critical point, where it is blocked by uncertainties.

Nishitani Keiji The Kyoto school reached its acme in Nishitani Keiji (1900–1990), a religious thinker who, with creative and tireless intellectual energy, spent his long life bringing the core issues of Eastern and Western philosophy into new perspective and expounding them in countless lectures and publications.[58] An early and active participant in congresses and symposia, he is largely responsible for the Kyoto school's outstanding place among the Eastern intellectual movements known in the West. The translation of his principal work, *Religion and Nothingness* (*Shūkyōto wa Nani ka*), placed him at the forefront of internationally known philosophers.[59] Always ready to enter into dialogue, Nishitani has enriched the East-West encounter with many new lines of thought. His painstaking efforts to acquire a penetrating personal grasp of Christianity made him one of the chief partners in the Buddhist-Christian dialogue.

Born in Ishikawa Prefecture, a stretch of coast on the rough Japan Sea, Nishitani was rooted in Japanese folk traditions. Unlike Nishida and Suzuki, Nishitani did not have a Zen Buddhist background. When he was very young, his family moved to Tokyo, where he completed his primary education. Then, as a pupil at the junior high school attached to Waseda University, he first came into contact with the Japanese world that was opening to the West. The school gave instruction in English language and literature and encouraged the pupils to appropriate European culture. In 1915 Nishitani's father died and he experienced sorrow for the first time.

From 1918 to 1921, he attended the prestigious Daiichi Kōtō-gakkō in Tokyo, which gladly opened its doors to the gifted boy. His studies there had a profound formative effect on the lively, high-spirited young man. In an autobiographical text, "My Youth" ("Watakushi no Seishun Jidai"), he speaks of these years as the happiest time of his life. Though surrounded by like-minded friends, he struggled alone toward an intellectual breakthrough, which was accompanied by great emotional tensions and crises. In his reminiscences he speaks of "boundless melancholy" and "deathly loneliness," motifs common to thoughtful and ambitious youths of all times.

His privileged schooling placed him among the intellectual elite of his country. Like most of his comrades, he was a passionate reader and acquired that broad knowledge of Western literature that astonished foreigners encountering the young Japanese intellectuals of those days. In Natsumi Sōseki, in particular, he found "a philosophical attitude and a Zen-like mood" that undoubtedly influenced his spiritual development. In a book stall near Yotsuya Station in Tokyo, he discovered a recently published work of a still little-known author, Nishida Kitarō. His thirst for knowledge prompted him to purchase the book, *Thought and Experience* (*Shisaku to Taiken*, 1915; Nishitani probably read the second edition of 1919). He had never read philosophy, which dominates the book's first section, and he found it unyielding despite his greatest efforts, but the essays on Tolstoy, Shinran, and Japanese literature in the second part deeply impressed him. His account of this decisive reading experience begins with these words: "I read Professor Nishida's *Thought and Experience*, and in the end this determined the course of my life." His heart was "deeply stirred." The great life questions that Nishida dealt with in his essays moved him strongly. When he turned to philosophy, Nishitani was concerned from the first with the problem of existence.

In 1921 he entered the philosophy department of Kyoto University and became Nishida's leading student. His biography details his student experiences and his impressions of Nishida. Especially interesting is Nishida's zeal for Zen, described by Nishitani in the memoir, "Nishida My Teacher" (1951).[60] Nishida practiced with great commitment under two famous Zen masters and sometimes even passed the night sitting in meditation on a stone in the mountains. As a high school student Nishitani had shown an early interest in Zen, reading a book of Zen texts collected by the founder of the Japanese

Ōbaku school, Ingen, from which he quoted in his final school composition.[61] But little is known of Nishitani's Zen practice. Though he carefully separated scholarship from praxis, we know that he devoted himself to Zen practice at the Engakuji in Kamakura and later at the Shōkokuji in Kyoto, where his master gave him the Dharma name "Sound of the Valley" (Japanese: *Keisei*), borrowed from a chapter in Dōgen's *Shōbōgenzō*.

Nishitani gives valuable autobiographical information and a sketch of his philosophical progress in a short text, "The Point of Departure of My Philosophy," which he composed in the year he retired from the professorship of philosophy of religion at Kyoto University, a position he held from 1943 to 1963. His grounding in Buddhism is attested by the statement: "Gradually I came to the point where I thought entirely in Buddhist categories." A few lines later he adds that, looking back, he sees this attraction to Buddhist thinking as evidence that such thinking was latent in him from the beginning, even before he began his philosophical studies.

He lists the literary figures that influenced his intellectual development before his acquaintance with Nishida: Nietzsche and Dostoevski, Emerson and Carlyle; he also mentions the Bible and St. Francis of Assisi and, from Japan, Natsume Sōseki (1867–1916) and the two Zen masters Hakuin (1685–1768) and Takuan (1573–1645). In this varied reading he was guided above all by the strongly felt pressure of the question of nihilism, which prompted his "doubt about the existence of the self, a doubt related to what in Buddhism is called the 'Great Doubt'." His interest in mysticism was aroused at an early date by Emerson. Schelling and Plotinus were a source of basic knowledge, and throughout his life he was strongly drawn to German mysticism, especially that of Meister Eckhart and Jacob Boehme. Among the favored authors of his youth he names Bergson and Kierkegaard, and later, Heidegger and Sartre. Nishitani sees as motivating his philosophy the need to overcome nihilism, understood not as a sense of the meaninglessness of life or as a philosophical ideology but as a personal challenge to his self. The point of departure of his philosophy is the existential "doubt at the base of human life," which is in his view the deepest level of nihilism. Through resolving this doubt and overcoming nihilism, he reached the metaphysics of *śūnyatā* and absolute nothingness, the core doctrines of the Mahāyāna *Wisdom Sutras* and of Zen.[62] Jan Van Bragt, the leading expert on Nishitani's thought, deduces from the passages we have cited that his entire oeuvre is an effort to create a fundamental theology for Zen Buddhism.[63] This judgment identifies the centrality of Buddhism and Zen in the philosopher's work, which aspires to a comprehensive view of Eastern and Western thought under the guidance of the Zen Buddhist standpoint.

In naming the confrontation with nihilism as the point of departure of his thinking, Nishitani explains that he means a radical nihilism that undermines the stability of the self, forcing us to pose anew the question of selfhood raised by the great of philosophers—in Socrates' "Know thyself," in Augustine's sense of the strategic role of self-knowledge that made him wish nothing else than to know God and the self, and finally in Descartes, who formulates the question of the self at the threshold of modern philosophy. Nishitani is aware that the question of self is just as important to Shākyamuni and early Buddhism, and he is aware also that the Zen disciple who embarks on the path to enlightenment is devoting himself to a search for self.

In the forceful essay "The Standpoint of Zen" Nishitani explains the significance of the question of the self in Eastern thought. To begin, he cites the saying of the famous Japanese Zen master and founder of the Daitōkuji in Kyoto, Daitō Kokushi (1281–1338), about the "study of self" (Japanese: *koji kyūmei*). "I think it most aptly indicates the unique character of the standpoint of Zen. Zen is that standpoint which exhaustively investigates the self itself. It is also spoken of as the way which sees through to the original face of the self." Nishitani distinguishes between the Eastern and the Western understandings of the self. In general, when people talk of the self, they mean the Western self-consciousness, shaped by rational thinking, which "internally makes itself into a screen, as it were, upon which it observes the stream of consciousness—the various sensations, emotions, desires, representations, conceptions." This thinking objectifies the self and places it over against God, the world, and every other reality, an opposition that underlies the dualism characteristic of Western thought. The Eastern self, on the contrary, is grounded in itself and transcends all human capacities and activities, especially consciousness, intellectual thinking, and representing. The self precedes all action and wards off all objectification. Resting on the non-self (Sanskrit: *anātman*), it is not confined to a subjective ego but is to be understood cosmocentrically as flowing from the All. In the mind, seen as the unifying force of consciousness and its activity, the self takes the central place; it is in the center of its own world and the world of all things. The self extends itself, viewed cosmically, out into the whole world. In this perspective "there is no fundamental difference between animals and human beings. Buddhism's view of humans as 'sentient beings' and hence as equal to all other animal species, derives from such a way of seeing." Nishitani then adds some thoughts on the "World-Soul" or "World-Spirit." The Great Doubt, which has a capital role in the Zen investigation of self, touches the self in its deepest ground and is essentially different from the methodical doubt of a Descartes in quest of an ultimate certitude. Descartes calls his investigations "meditations" in order to emphasize their difference from ordinary logical inquiries. In this context he puts forward the striking insight *Cogito, ergo sum*, regarded as fundamental to modern philosophy and discussed again and again by the major philosophers. It is clear that here Descartes leaves behind the way of logical inference. The *ergo* indicates a breakthrough that Nishitani regards as comparable to the break-through of Zen experience. However—and this is the decisive critique of the Japanese philosopher—Descartes quickly returns to the rational, logical Western way of thinking. He turns the experience into a basis for argumentation. His knowledge remains in the cognitive realm. In contrast, the Great Doubt of Zen involves the entire person in an existential way. It is "a doubt which grips one's whole body-mind, in which the self and all other things in their entirety become one big question mark." Unlike Descartes's doubt, which strives for argumentative certainty, the aim of the Great Doubt is not any philosophical knowledge but a total breakthrough, through which the self turns back to the true original self, without any influence from the outside, solely on the basis of the realization of immediate experience.[64]

Nishitani calls the Western self "self-centered" or "ego-centered," while the Eastern self is "cosmo-centered." One who has attained enlightenment in the breakthrough of the Great Doubt, through practical koan exercises, experiences himself in the unity of the cosmos and sees things "just as they are" (Japanese: *ari no mama*)—a phrase of rich connotations of which Nishitani is fond. The self is a center, linked with all things and open on every side. Nishitani touches on the theme of self-discovery in many writings, particularly suggestively in his short essay on "The Awakening of the Self in Buddhism," in which he praises the awakening of the true self to the original Dharma-nature as the essential fruit of the Buddhist religion.[65] Through Buddhism, he says, the self awakens to a realm beyond the world. Self-discovery brings about the deepest and most radical triumph over nihilism—this is perhaps Nishitani's most important philosophical insight.

A glance through Nishitani's numerous writings reveals that the confrontation with and eventual success in overcoming nihilism is the central theme that comes to complete maturation in the Zen Buddhist perspective. The essays selected from his early writings and published in two large volumes under the title *Philosophy of Fundamental Subjectivity* show his intense preoccupation with European philosophy.[66] It is the task of research on Nishitani to find in these essays the seeds of his final victory over nihilism. Let us note merely the outstanding place that these early works already give to religion. He is ultimately a religious philosopher, not merely an inquirer into the philosophy of the religions. The characteristic mark of his position is precisely his refusal to admit the validity of a distinction that would separate philosophy and religion.

In 1949 Nishitani, now middle-aged, published a conclusive, clearly structured work recently translated as *The Self-Overcoming of Nihilism*.[67] The work is a fulfillment of the author's youthful ambition to overcome nihilism through nihilism. This task had taken concrete shape in the course of his professional philosophical study. He saw the danger of nihilism to the European spirit but discerned a point at which a positively oriented, creative, and triumphant nihilism draws near to Buddhist insights. His exemplary presentation of Nietzsche's philosophy, which is not inferior to the Western literature on Nietzsche, need not occupy us here. What is new and exciting is the uncovering of the spiritual level at which affinities with Buddhism appear. The final chapter of the book, on the meaning of nihilism for us, opens access to a perspective embracing East and West, anticipating the decisive chapter of *Religion and Nothingness*.

45

After discussing the forms and contents of European nihilism, Nishitani poses the question of the significance of the positive form of European nihilism for Japanese culture, which, shaken in its traditional foundations and threatened by the progress of secularism, has entered a dangerous crisis. "The various manifestations of culture at present, if looked at closely, are mere shadows floating over the void." Historical changes have brought about "the greatest spiritual crisis." During the Meiji period there were strong personalities who were animated by traditional Far Eastern culture and assumed a role of leadership, but only after a loss of moral energy caused the culture to sink into a vacuum, according to Nishitani.

Nishitani sums up the present task of Japanese philosophy, as revealed by the study of European nihilism, under three headings that throw a strong light on his philosophical ethos. The first two involve becoming aware of the vacuum Japan faces and arousing the will to overcome it. A look at Western cultural history can help here. Though Nishitani values the prophetic power of Nietzsche and Kierkegaard, he warns that the study of European philosophy must not lead to the destruction of Japan's own traditions. "European nihilism teaches us to return to our forgotten selves and to reflect on the tradition of Oriental culture. This tradition is lost to us at present and we must rediscover it." It is not a question of a return to the past, to archaic, exhausted forms, but of a reawakening. Nishitani points to the active, positive effort to overcome nihilism in Europe and calls on his compatriots to do likewise and to engage themselves with Far Eastern culture, especially the Buddhist standpoints of emptiness (Japanese: *kū*; Sanskrit: *śūnyatā*) and nothingness (Japanese: *mu*). This mutual mediation of past and future can make possible a spiritual awakening.[68]

In regarding tradition as the antidote to nihilism, Nishitani has in mind above all Japan's Buddhist heritage, though he values

Japanese religion in all its forms, including Shinto. Buddhism has had a normative place in the philosophical realm since the beginnings of the Kyoto school. Nishitani would have liked to substantiate from the European side his surmise of a direct link between European nihilism and the Mahāyāna school, but the inadequate knowledge and, still more, the limited understanding of Buddhism among the German philosophers of the nineteenth and the first half of the twentieth centuries offered no firm points of contact for the two traditions. Nishitani recognizes Schopenhauer's deep interest in Buddhism, but this does not constitute a genuine link; quotations from Nietzsche reveal how thoroughly this philosopher misunderstood Buddhism. Clearly, there is no organic link from this phase of German philosophy to Nishitani's Mahāyāna Buddhist ideas. He quotes two texts that he sees as significant for the triumph over nihilism in Mahāyāna, one from a tract of the Indian philosopher Nāgārjuna and the other from the collected sayings of the Chinese Zen master Lin-chi, known as the *Rinzairoku* in Japan. Thus he comes to the threshold of his great work, *Religion and Nothingness*, which presents his own original philosophical vision and a complete overcoming of nihilism.

In *The Self-Overcoming of Nihilism*, Nishitani presented modern Western efforts to overcome nihilism, in particular those of Stirner, Nietzsche, Heidegger, and Sartre. These philosophers addressed the sense of the meaninglessness of existence that so oppresses many people. They were able to break through their consciousness of self and to find at its root a fundamental nihilism, which they reached in an "ecstatic transcendence."

Nishitani underscores the difference between this kind of nihilism and the Far Eastern Nothingness to which the Buddhist realm of emptiness opens access. Sartre, the Western nihilist, tried to escape from the prison of the *cogito*: "The standpoint of the ego is constituted

47

by a duplication of the *cogito* in which the *cogito* is considered from the viewpoint of the *cogito* itself. This leads to subjectivity becoming a self shut up within itself: the self is bound up by itself in such a way that it cannot extricate itself from itself. The very existence of this self is marked by a 'self- attachment,' as if one had tied one's hands with one's own rope."[69] But Sartre's ecstatic transcendence is no escape: "He recognizes a transcendence here that is a form of *ekstasis*: a standing-outside-of-oneself. . . . This transcendence means that nothingness is constituted at the ground of self-existence. . . . But insofar as Sartre locates subjectivity at the standpoint of the Cartesian ego, his nothingness is not even the 'death' of which Heidegger speaks. . . . Nor is it anything like the Great Doubt . . . since the Great Doubt signals nothing less than the bankruptcy of the Cartesian ego. Even less are we dealing here with the Buddhist notion of *śūnyatā*." Sartre regards nothingness "like a wall at the bottom of the ego or like a springboard underfoot of the ego. This turns his nothingness into a basic principle that shuts the ego up within itself."[70] Nietzsche, more penetratingly, sees nihility "as the field of the ecstatic transcendence of human existence, that is, the field on which human Existenz comes into being. It is on this field that Existenz assumes responsibility for creating new meanings for the meaningless and nihility of life and existence." He strives for a humanism that can "affirm life in all its absurdity" and erects as its goal "the image of the 'Overman' or the image of the fully human 'man.'"[71]

Undoubtedly the nihilistic currents in modern Western philosophy have greatly contributed to the mechanization of modern man. "Eventually the field on which the machine comes into being—referred to above as a field of mutual alliance between abstract intellect in quest of scientific rationality and denaturalized nature—discloses nihility both at the ground of man which relies on that intellect and at the ground of the world of nature." Dehumanization occurs as "a fundamental intertwining of the mechanization of man and his transformation into a subject in pursuit of its desires, at the ground of which nihility has opened up as a sense of the meaninglessness of the whole business."[72] What is the way out of this situation? "Talk of a world order dependent on God, of a providence in history, and even of the very existence of God has become alien to the mind of man. Man grows increasingly indifferent to such notions as these and eventually to his own humanness as well." In these desperate straits one seeks a place of spiritual freedom: "At this point the demand arises for a transpersonal field to open up—beyond the standpoint of personality or spirit, and yet the only sort of field on which personality and spirit can become manifest." Nishitani finds a place of this kind in the *Abgeschiedenheit* (detachment, retirement) of Meister Eckhart, to whose deep religious insights he attaches great importance: "Eckhart pointed to such a standpoint in explaining the 'essence' of the personal God as absolute nothingness. . . . The 'detachment' that Eckhart spoke of as a radical departure not only from self and world but even from 'God'—the flight from God for the sake of God—must rest, as it were, in an absolutely transcendent near side. . . . In the Buddhist standpoint of *śūnyatā* (emptiness), this point comes to light still more clearly. *Śūnyatā* is the point at which we become manifest in our own suchness as concrete human beings, as individuals with both body and personality. And at the same time, it is the point at which everything around us becomes manifest in its own suchness."[73]

Emptiness (*śūnyatā*) is a core concept of Mahāyāna, central to the work of the great Indian Buddhist philosopher Nāgārjuna and his school of the "middle way" (Mādhyamika). The multifaceted concept

49

is equally central for Nishitani, who highlights those aspects that seem important for the confrontation with Western nihilism. Western nihilist philosophy, too, is able to surpass the everyday ego and the apparent meaninglessness of ordinary existence, but in its "ecstatic transcendence" it remains tied to the self and tends to objectify nothingness as a thing that is not, or an entity that is negated and that is outside real being. This philosophy does not open itself to the unrestricted space and freedom that alone manifests the complete victory over nihilism.

Śūnyatā, as Buddhist philosophy makes clear, is not a "something" belonging to the register of being and non-being but transcends all contraries and distinctions. Nishitani shows the fundamental distinction between the nothingness of Western nihilism and the field of emptiness. "Emptiness in the sense of *śūnyatā* is emptiness only when it empties itself even of the standpoint that represents it as some 'thing' that is emptiness." Emptiness is tied neither to being nor non-being; it leads into a realm that is deeper than the abyss of Western nihilism, namely, into the bottomless depth of sameness; here all things exist in absolute self-identity on the plane of equality, "an absolute self-identity in which the one and the other are yet truly themselves, at once absolutely broken apart and absolutely joined together. They are an absolute *two* and at the same time an absolute *one*. In the words of the Zen master Daitō Kokushi (1282–1338): 'Separated from one another by a hundred million kalpas, yet not apart a single moment; sitting face-to-face all day long, yet not opposed for an instant.'" Nishitani also quotes the verse of the Japanese Zen master Gasan Jōseki (1275–1365):

> The heart and mind of this shadowy man
> At all occasions is to me most familiar—
> From long ago so mysteriously wondrous,
> It is neither I nor other.

The last line reveals emptiness as the place of sameness, where emptiness, in order to become true emptiness, is emptied and everything appears in its true, real thusness.[74]

In the field of emptiness, all the nihility of Western nihilism is completely overcome. Eastern philosophy shows itself on this point to be a philosophy of affirmation. A summary in Nishitani's work closes with the near-triumphal sentences: "On that field of *śūnyatā* each thing becomes manifest in its suchness in its very act of affirming itself, according to its own particular potential and *virtus* and its own particular shape. For us as human beings, to revert to that field entails at one and the same time an elemental affirmation of the existence of all things (the world) and an elemental affirmation of our own existence. The field of *śūnyatā* is nothing other than the field of the Great Affirmation."[75]

In presenting the *śūnyatā* philosophy, Nishitani is not satisfied with overcoming Western nihilism: the place of emptiness, the center of his effort of thought, is grounded in the Mahāyāna sutras and reflects the outlook of Zen. Many Zen koans owe their cutting edge to the dialectic of the *Perfection of Wisdom Sutras*, and their relation to the *Avatamsaka Sutra* is equally important. The mutual unity of being and emptiness and the reciprocal interlinking of all things are important themes in the *Avatamsaka Sutra* and common in Zen as a whole. The philosophy at the base of Zen and Nishitani's central thoughts spring from the same roots.

Nishitani gives a modern twist to Buddhist themes by his focus on the problem of nihilism, which he sees as "the essential characteristic of modern civilization."[76] It is this nihilistic streak in Western culture that creates the apparent conflict between science and religion: "I am convinced that the problem of nihilism lies at the root of the mutual distaste between religion and science."[77] On the religious side, the hostility arises because science has destroyed the teleological

51

world view based on faith in providence and in a divine governance of the world.

Nishitani, who dealt with the theme of religion and science from an early date, frequently points out this connection, in various chapters of *Religion and Nothingness*, for example, and at length in an essay, "Science and Zen."[78] According to traditional religions, the ordered structure of the world rests on laws of nature directed toward a goal; these laws reveal to believers the wisdom and omnipotence of the Creator. In contrast, modern science investigates the intrinsic laws of the world, the impersonal, dead mechanism at work in it, which has no relation to humans or to the human environment. The mechanical scientific worldview, according to its proponents, is proven by exact research. Nishitani, too, sees it as an indubitable fact, and he sees efforts to unite the mechanical with the teleological worldview as futile. Reality, just as it is, presents contradictory aspects on the rational plane, which religious thinkers also recognize and which they should seek to understand through deeper insight. In addition, the exact sciences can help a religion open to modern knowledge to purge itself of anthropomorphic representations.

As in the victory over nihilism, Nishitani here invokes the way of negativity. Where the teleological worldview indicates the ascending line from matter through life to humanity and its Creator, modern science reveals a line that descends from matter to dissolution by way of mechanical analysis. To reconcile these aspects at a fundamental level requires a thought process corresponding to the philosophy of emptiness. Nishitani follows such a process in his essay on the field of the "unground" or groundlessness or nothingness as the background of the world; this is made possible by a turnabout in the realization of the Great Death. In this field, the ascending and descending lines, the teleological and mechanical, converge; the field of nothingness transcends both sides, matter as well as life and mind:

"the truth itself rather demands a single vision that can grasp both sides simultaneously."[79] The *śūnyatā* philosophy permits the dissolution of the apparent conflict between religion and science, as Nishitani shows through koan-like Zen sayings. His demythologizing existentialist interpretation of the koans raises to a higher level the contradictory aspects of reality that they represent. The apparently nonsensical koan that has "a wooden man sing and a stone woman dance" concerns the world neither in its living, teleological aspect nor in its material, mechanical aspect but points to a world that surpasses these ways of seeing, in which irreconcilable aspects are mutually penetrating and are subsumed.[80] Such an interpretation differs from the usual account of the struggle with the koan as a means of suppressing logical thinking, in that it has recourse to the existentialist logic of the *śūnyatā* philosophy.

Nishitani's view of modern science from this philosophical perspective testifies to his effort to do justice to contemporary questions. The spirit of Zen is shown in his fidelity to immediate experience, which is as attentive to the scientific as to the Zen world. "The uniqueness of Zen is the combination of its religious character and the stress on immediacy in terms of experience."[81] Despite the rapprochement of Eastern and Western thought, a doubt remains as to whether such philosophizing can adequately address the human problems arising from the extraordinary progress of modern science. In accepting the disappearance of teleology as a success of modern science, Nishitani leaves himself open to justified criticism. The epochal shift brought about by science and technology probably cannot be accommodated by traditional philosophical categories, whether Eastern or Western. For all the acumen and modernity of his discussion of religion and science, it is just here that we recognize the limits of Nishitani's philosophy.

Ueda Shizuteru Among the many pupils of Nishitani who today form the core of the Kyoto school, Ueda Shizuteru (b. 1926) stands out. Under Nishitani's guidance, he studied philosophy of religion at Kyoto University and, after earning his doctorate, continued his studies in Germany, as his teacher had done, finally taking over Nishitani's chair in 1976. Ueda was raised a Buddhist, and during his years of study he steeped himself in the spirit of the Kyoto school. He too seeks a synthesis of Western thought and Mahāyāna metaphysics in the concrete form of Zen, appropriating Nishitani's *śūnyatā* philosophy and admiring Nishida's pioneering achievement in bridging the chasm between the pure experience articulated in Zen and philosophical reflection. The results of his scholarly efforts are found in his very fine German doctoral dissertation for the University of Marburg and in numerous essays that develop the themes of the dissertation to build up a coherent and thoroughly developed doctrine. A major work of synthesis is confidently expected of this tirelessly creative scholar, who was named emeritus in 1990—early by the standards of Japanese state universities.

His doctoral dissertation, *The Birth of God in the Soul and the Breakthrough to Godhead: Meister Eckhart's Mystical Anthropology and its Confrontation with the Mysticism of Zen Buddhism*, forms the basis of the later philosophical investigations. The choice of theme is in the tradition of the Kyoto school, going back to Nishida's discovery of spiritual affinities between Zen and German mysticism. Nishitani, too, composed a significant monograph on Eckhart, under the title *Absolute Nothingness*. Ueda was guided in his Eckhart studies by Friedrich Heiler, the veteran of the science of religions, who had a special interest in mysticism, and by Ernst Benz, who had made his name with a work on Eckhart. If we look to Ueda's dissertation for an account of his understanding of Zen and especially of the philosophy that underlies and pervades Zen, we will not be disappointed.

As Ueda sees it, Eckhart's inner religious experience is expressed in the themes of the birth of God and the breakthrough to the Godhead, which he carefully examines in the two parts of the thesis. The first of these leaps into the deep mysteries of the Trinity and the Incarnation. "God gives birth to his Son in the soul and thereby to the soul as his Son." Ueda points out that the Christian mysteries, like the Zen experience, are ineffable. Eckhart holds fast to the unity of the three-personed God: they are "one undivided God (*unus indivisus Deus*)" or utterly "one thing." Ueda, like many Eckhart scholars, believes that this concentration on the One reveals Neo-Platonic influences. Though this cannot be denied, Ueda's further discussions, which trace parallels to the Zen way, reveal how much Eckhart distanced himself from the speculative philosophy of the Neo-Platonists in teaching a Zen-like spirituality for everyday life in the world. Bold formulas such as "man became God" or "the divine man" (*homo divinus*) remain, like the language of the Greek fathers about the "divinization" of human beings, within the framework of Christian orthodoxy. Ueda agrees, but he demurs when Eckhart in his German sermons seems to equate the birth of God in the soul with the event of the Incarnation.

Eckhart takes from Augustine the idea of the soul as capable of receiving God (*capax Dei*), but he is not content to derive from the birth of God in the soul only a union of the soul with God, in which the soul lives the life of God and cooperates with God; in the theme of the breakthrough, the inner dynamic of his thought pushes further. The soul desires to break through God to reach the ground of God, which is the Godhead. In this distinction between God and the Godhead, the Godhead is God's innermost essence, a purity beyond all relations, "the still desert into which no distinction has ever crept, neither Father nor Son nor Holy Spirit." This creates a difficulty of interpretation. Yet, as Ueda remarks, this pressing forward to the

One did not lead "to a complete dissolution of the notion of the Trinity." According to Eckhart, the soul, through its ground, breaks through to the ground of God, the Godhead. The soul's ground, or the divine spark, is one with the ground of God. Ueda remarks: "The identity of the ground of the soul with the ground of God is something completely different from the identity of the soul with God." The experience of breakthrough can be compared with the psychological phenomenon of Zen enlightenment.

Also important for the confrontation with Zen are Eckhart's utterances on the divine nothingness, which belong to the tradition of negative theology that reaches back to early Christianity and first found expression in the fifth-century Christian Neo-Platonist Pseudo-Dionysius. The German sermons refer often and enthusiastically to the divine nothingness, applying the terminology of "nothing" and "beyond" to God and the Godhead. One sermon ends as follows: "You should love him as he is a non-God, a non-Spirit, a non-person, a non-image, and still more, a pure One cut off from all duality. And in this One we should sink for ever from something to nothing. May God help us in so to do. Amen." He takes Acts 9.8—"when his eyes were opened, he could see nothing"—as indicating that God is at once a nothing and a something (*ein Nicht und ein Icht*), a nothingness beyond being and an utterly transcendent being. Ueda deals at length with Eckhart's comments that "God is a true light that shines in the darkness" (cf. John 1.5,9) in terms of three darknesses, of which the third is the best: "it is the concealed darkness of the eternal Godhead, which is unknown and was never known and in which God remains in himself unknown; the light of the eternal Father has eternally shone into it, but the darkness does not grasp the light." Ueda explains this obscure text as meaning that the darkness of the Godhead embraces the light of God. "The nothingness, which God in himself is, lies beyond every opposition of God and creature or of God and humans; it is neither being nor nothingness." However Eckhart's bold statements are to be interpreted, his utterance about nothingness has a parallel in the thunderous shout of the fourth Chinese Zen Patriarch Tao-hsin (580–651) about "the nothingness of the Buddha-nature," which was orchestrated by Dōgen in his chapter on the Buddha-nature and which still echoes in many Zen halls. Both traditions repel equally strongly all rationalization and verbalization, although on different metaphysical premises.

The Mahāyāna doctrine of emptiness, radically understood by Zen practitioners as the emptying out of all thought and representation, all will and desire, corresponds to Eckhart's call to complete detachment as the necessary precondition for the union of the soul with God. His sermons drive home this necessity with inexhaustible verbal invention: humans must be silent, blind, deaf, dwell in poverty and solitude, even die, leaving all things and their own selves to be free and pure, leaving God for the sake of God and entering into darkness and night. "You must be quite still and wait in his pure nothingness." This is Eckhart's "fundamental death," which is close to the Great Death of Zen experience. Detachment and serenity (*Gelassenheit*) resemble the stilling of all mental activities, toward the condition of emptiness sought in Zen practice. Zen, according to Ueda, goes beyond the degree of emptying demanded by Eckhart only insofar as it demands the emptying of emptiness itself, so that it is not an emptiness with a view to receiving something, but utter emptiness. Eckhart's desert of detachment is a place open for God and the Godhead.

Both in his Eckhart book and his essay, Ueda goes to great pains to demonstrate that Eckhart's spiritual path is an ascending one, from the Christ-mysticism of the birth of God in the soul, via the God-mysticism of the breakthrough to Godhead, to the overcoming of mysticism—that is, to a state of being-in-the-world, which, like the emptying of Zen, is again surpassed. "At its highest Eckhart's mysticism is no longer mysticism." This is correct, but so is what follows: "the idea of pure being-one with the pure One is not carried to its last consequence by Eckhart, namely, to a dissolution of Christian concepts and Christian piety." The one who has attained union with God turns to the reality of the world. Eckhart, as is well known, urged that one should immediately abandon even the state of highest contemplation to meet the needs of a hungry beggar. This aspect of his teaching sheds light on his original reading of the story of Mary and Martha (Luke 10.38–42). He notes and praises Martha's work in the kitchen: "she lived long and well." Though busy with many things, working from the ground of the soul, she found God in all. The active life, as Eckhart understands it, is not separate from the contemplative one. The true, detached man sees God in all things. The complete binding of the active with the contemplative life is to be striven for as the highest stage on the way to union with God.

In the summary of his book, Ueda notes "remarkable points in common" and even a "certain essential affinity" with Zen Buddhism but adds that "the return to worldly reality as the practical completion of the breakthrough to true transcendence . . . is carried out in Zen Buddhism far more radically and more consequently." "Eckhart could not draw the ultimate consequences, nor did he want to." Ueda accordingly concludes: "This short comparison with Zen Buddhism thus shows the mysticism of Meister Eckhart to be inseparable from the Christian foundation; it is a Christian mysticism although within Christianity it represents a radical deviation from church orthodoxy."[82]

In several essays in German, Ueda seeks to make the spiritual proximity of Eckhart to Zen more palpable and to grasp the differences more sharply. To this end, he employs the last three of the ten pictures in the series called *The Ox and its Owner*.[83] In a penetrating lecture to the Eranos Society, he presents these three pictures as "an illustration of the movement of the true self." The first picture, the empty circle, signifies absolute nothingness, the total negation of every kind of duality. One must leap into pure nothingness, undergo the Great Death. The second picture, a blossoming tree by a river, is neither an objective nor a metaphorical landscape but makes present in an unobjectified way the selflessness and freedom of the true person. The third picture, of an old man meeting a young one, signifies the selfless self-unfolding of the old man in the interstice— the "between"—of the I-Thou. In summary, "It is an encounter which reveals that existence is accompanied by an invisible circle of communication between nothingness and nature."

How, or at what point, can Eckhart's thinking be inserted into the movement captured in the three pictures? The empty circle, suitably interpreted, could symbolize his negative theology. But for Eckhart the nothingness of God is at the same time transcendent being, the supreme actuality of being, whereas the emptiness of Zen, the absolute nothingness of emptied emptiness, is neither being nor non-being. The Zen negation is more radical. While Eckhart's ascending negation leads to the complete emptying of all things and of self, and to leaving God to the nothingness of the Godhead, "the infinity of negation" in Zen aims at "the infinite nothingness 'beyond the hundredfold negation'." The nothingness of Zen is neither being nor non-being; yet it is not a nihilistic nothingness, but a simultaneous negation and affirmation. The empty circle is the image of this "simultaneity" and "neither/nor," the "Mahāyāna Buddhist thinking of all relations." Relation is the basic concept of Mahāyāna philosophy, according to which all things (Dharma), along with the ego, are a radically desubstantialized reality; they both are and are not. Eckhart's negative theology does not go this far. This indicates the limit of the relevance of the second picture for Eckhart's thought. The blossoming tree by the river, interpreted as nature in its thusness, as "things just as they are," indicates no transparence to the transcendent. Zen affirms all things in an unmediated way, "the mountains as mountains, the waters as waters." In contrast, Eckhart in turning to nature and the world never forgets the grounding of all being in God. "If all creatures 'are green' in God, then that is Eckhart's affirmation of the flea, and indeed as a flea in God." The difference is unmistakable.

The eighth and ninth ox pictures represent the coincidence in Zen of the radical negation of emptiness and the highest affirmation of the actual. The Chinese text carries the inscriptions "Both forgotten" (namely, ox and owner, hence emptiness) and "Returned to ground and origin": "the river flows as it flows, the flower blooms as it blooms." We could find Eckhartian correspondences for both pictures, but a difference remains, based in Eckhart's Christian standpoint. We leave Ueda's Zen-Christian comparison with his account of the tenth picture, though all his work has a connection with Christianity in a broad sense. Ueda's interpretation of this picture deviates in an original way from the traditional one. The Chinese inscription reads "Coming home from the market place with open hands." The usual explanation is that the enlightened one, having returned to everyday life, generously gives gifts, or in Buddhist terms, leads erring beings to liberating enlightenment in the manner of a Bodhisattva. But Ueda starts from the "between" of the encounter between the two men in the picture: Against the selfless self-unfolding represented by the old man, the young man becomes the locus of the existential question about the self, so that between the two the question and answer game of a koan can arise, for instance: "Where do you come from?" "What is your name?"—everyday questions that in Zen become questions about the original face, the true reality, the self of the other. A place for the relation to the other opens up but, as Ueda emphasizes, "no longer in a subject-object framework, and also not quite in the same way as Martin Buber's 'I and Thou,' though the I-Thou relationship is contained in it as a scientific moment."

This interpretation tells us much about Ueda's understanding of Zen. He is also concerned with Zen practice: the same lecture deals penetratingly with the basic exercises of zazen and the koan. Zazen is "sitting as Zen" and "Zen as sitting." In the individual elements of the exercise, he discovers essential components of Zen. He sees zazen as "bodily expression and accomplishment of still recollection and serene openness." The practitioner must "let what is thus recollected be penetrated by boundless openness." Ueda sets zazen in relation to the question-and-answer dialogue of the koan, seeing it as "the embodiment of the radical placing in question of the person through the basic question and its insolubility. . . . But it is at the same time the embodiment of the answer, the solvedness." He devotes special attention to the relation to the other that the koan dialogue brings to the fore. Whereas Buber's "I and Thou" looks through the relation with the other to the "eternal Thou," in Zen "I and Thou . . . are pervaded by the neither-I-nor-Thou that appears at the unground in the depths of zazen. Thus the between of I and Thou has become the un-grounding groundlessness of the depths." Classical koan examples show how in the encounter with the partner (an encounter of self with self), each puts the other in question, and in the play of question and answer even duality disappears in an utter affirmation, often expressed in a gesture, a thunderous shout, or a resonant laugh.[84]

A lengthy essay, "Nichijō Kūfu" ("Everyday Practice" or, as Ueda would translate it, "The Everyday as Practice"), begins with an account of the basic meaning of zazen, which allows one to master all the circumstances of the everyday and which leads, without set intent, to the origin, to "the great, definitive, fundamental conversion."[85] For the original person in freedom, "the everyday is immediately Zen" and "Zen is immediately the everyday." Ueda develops Zen ascesis in the everyday in two directions, the ascending line from the everyday to Zen, in which the practitioner makes all the details of the ordinary into Zen, and the descending line from Zen to the ordinary, in which the things of the everyday are affirmed in their everydayness by the Zen person and used so that they are of service to others. In practice, the two lines coincide and are anchored in zazen.

Ueda, himself linguistically gifted, made an important contribution to the understanding of Zen in terms of philosophy of language. He sees in the koan and the *mondō* (question and answer) an exemplary form of human dialogue. The *mondō* is unique to Zen and is quite distinct from other forms of religious verbal expression, as Ueda illustrates.[86] If one takes the core proposition of Mahāyāna philosophy, "One is many; many is one," and makes it into a *mondō*— "What is one? Many." "What is many? One."—the thesis presented in the proposition becomes a question-and-answer game charged with dynamism through the human beings that participate. A person is a living self whose question aims at the self of the partner. In this simplest of exchanges is revealed the essence of the Zen *mondō*, which is always concerned with the "original face," the "true self." In such dialogues the master asks (usually in some precise context), "Who are you?"—that is, he asks about the self of his interlocutor. The disciple likewise asks the master, "Who am I?," that is, "What is my self?" This basic structure is varied in many ways. In the *mondō* of the one and the many, the answer can easily be stated as a proposition. In other koans, the answer seems quite disconnected from the context: "What is the Buddha? A pound of hemp." "What is the meaning of the coming of the First Patriarch (Bodhidharma) from the West? The tree in the courtyard."[87] Arranged as propositions, these exchanges make no sense.

Though Zen hates verbalization and prides itself on transmission without words, it has, paradoxically, produced an extraordinary wealth of literature. Ueda aims to discover a primordial or fundamental word, which is preceded by an original silence. He quotes the words in which Nishida summed up his entire enterprise: "I would like to try to clarify everything in the light of the claim that pure experience is the only real reality." Ueda finds here "a threefold process that in turn represents a manifold of different levels: (1) pure experience, (2) pure experience as the only real reality, and (3) clarifying everything in the light of the claim that pure experience is the only real reality." Linguistically, (1) presents pure experience as an event, hidden ineffably like the original word in the original silence. In (2) this experience produces a reflexive, epistemic formulation of its identity, "pure experience as the only real reality," and is thus caught in a net of words that can be woven and rewoven, opening up the possibility of a Zen literature. In (3), "the phrase 'pure experience' is already a philosophical term and loses its distinctive Zen character."[88]

Ueda is familiar with Western philosophies of language and in this context mentions Humboldt, Cassirer, Bollnow, Jaspers, and Heidegger. He finds a resonance with the Far Eastern understanding of language in Merleau-Ponty's phenomenology of language, which goes beyond institutionalized and utilitarian language to the creative word and discovers a "primordial silence" under the noise of the many words. The breakthrough to this silence releases a deep movement affecting not only language but the human person, bringing about what the French philosopher calls "a modulation of my own existence" and "a transformation of my own being."[89]

In his book on Eckhart, Ueda comments lovingly on the poem of Angelus Silesius, "The rose is without why, it blossoms for it blossoms."[90] The "without why" illuminates for him ultimate metaphysical connections. It is also his final explanation of language. The primordial word is "without why." He draws on another famous rose poem, Rilke's epitaph: "Rose, oh pure contradiction, the pleasure to be nobody's sleep under so many lids."[91] In this poem, the "oh" is the numinous primordial sound, which contains the following words *in nuce*. In this word, "pure experience" (Nishida) is present. Pure experience and fundamental word are event, presence, "without why," beyond every distinction, and unobjectified. Ueda's philosophy of language travels in the same place as unobjectified Zen meditation.

Like his teacher Nishitani, Ueda is concerned with the problematic of the technological age, but instead of seeking the solution in a metaphysics of *śūnyatā*, he faces in its full extent the danger of secularization that threatens all religion today. In a contribution to a Salzburg symposium, "Has Religion a Future?," in which he addresses "The Contemporary Spiritual Situation of Japan" from a Zen perspective, he first notes that for the founder Shākyamuni and the monastic orders he instituted, secularization was not a problem, since the monks had totally abandoned house and world and rejected all social ties. A certain tension between "leaving the world" and "staying in the world" first appears in Mahāyāna. Refusing to recognize any separation between this-worldly and other-worldly, between *samsāra* and nirvana, and abolishing the distinction between sacred and profane, Mahāyāna removes the basis in East Asian Buddhism for the problem of secularism, namely, the transition from the sacred to the profane. In a universe characterized by the Zen saying "Open space—nothing holy," there is simply no room for a process of secularization.

However, the Mahāyāna openness to the world, unlike the ascetic rejection of the world in Theravāda Buddhism, promotes the investigation of certain phenomena of secularization. Ueda sees the basic Mahāyāna idea of return to the world without distinction of sacred and profane as realized in classical Zen. Thus "the simplest everyday or worldly activities such as tea-drinking, writing characters, etc., are deepened in Mahāyāna Buddhism into the 'way' of tea, the 'way' of writing, in that in each case the activity is transformed into an activity performed as something arising from meditative absorption . . . without on the one hand abandoning the absorption nor on the other adding anything special to the worldly activity." Ueda's judgment is confirmed by what one knows of the culture of enlightened masters. But Ueda is aware of the danger posed by this fusion of enlightenment and the worldly, and he deplores bitterly the decline into worldliness of wide circles of Japanese Buddhism: "Buddhism is in a difficult, a very difficult situation," for it finds itself "perhaps for the first time in its history in a fundamentally alien world. . . . Buddhism with its openness for the world now wanders emptily in the technological world." The Buddhist image of man with the ideal of overcoming ego sees itself faced with a measureless expansion of the ego. Here Ueda sees clearly the crisis of religion, including Buddhism, and of humanity in the technological world.

Yet he can also discern a good side to the global process of secularization that today seeks to free every domain of life from religious influence. Such pressures send religions back to their own, original reality. To the religiously grounded understanding of nature central to Far Eastern culture, the West has added science and technology, thus allowing penetrating analysis and a clearer differentiation of subjective and objective. Though the dualism of subject and object is foreign to the Far Eastern sense of nature, Ueda points out that this does not indicate any lack of rational capacity in Asians, and that "there are many things of importance to humanity that are not to be learnt rationally." The undeniable value of non-objectified experience is also being appreciated anew today in the West.[92]

THE ZEN PHILOSOPHY AND THE EAST-WEST ENCOUNTER

The philosophical ferment that has been a part of Buddhism since its beginnings has entered a new phase with the encounter between Zen and Western philosophy, thanks in large measure to the Kyoto school. Though philosophical elements have appeared elsewhere in Zen, the Kyoto school is so well known that some have identified it as representing Japanese Zen Buddhism, ignoring the vitality of the numerous temples and monasteries in which meditation is regularly and zealously practiced with no reference to the intellectual concerns of the Kyoto philosophers.

The Kyoto school's place at the forefront of Japanese Buddhism is based on the fact that in it, for the first time, Zen arrives at full philosophical reflection. A second factor that gives the school special significance for the West is its readiness for exchanges with thinkers of other cultures. An extensive literature records the fruits of such contacts with Heiler, Benz, Heidegger, Tillich, Toynbee, and others. Their awareness of the importance of the religious dimension has brought the Kyoto philosophers into a dialogue with Christianity inspired less by ecumenism than by the search for truth and wisdom. This dialogue is exemplified by a symposium held in 1980 at the Nanzan Institute for Religion and Culture on "Absolute Nothingness and God: The Nishida-Tanabe Tradition and Christianity."[93] Three of the philosophers discussed above (Takeuchi, Nishitani, and Ueda), together with Christian theologians, inquired into the significance of Nishida's and Tanabe's thought for the Buddhist-Christian dialogue. The fruitful debate justified Jan Van Bragt's opening declaration that the philosophy of the Kyoto school provided a unique platform for the intensive and scholarly encounter of Christian and Buddhist theologians.

The philosophy of Zen—not that of the Kyoto school alone, but the philosophical tendency inherent in Zen—tackles central human problems in a manner that appeals to modern culture.[94] It deals with the ontological problems of being and time, reality and conscious-ness, and the anthropological problems of the meaning of human life and the interrelationships of body and soul, life and death; it roots these concerns in a practice inspired by existential anxiety and care and directed toward definitive liberation and salvation. A fruit of the Buddhist path of salvation, this philosophy grew out of the Mahāyāna sutras, whose philosophical content is still by no means fully clarified or exhausted, and was enriched in its Chinese phase by an influx of Taoist wisdom. It is remarkable that in the history of the movement, the strongest and most original masters—a Lin-chi or a Dōgen—were also those who, through their creative use of dialectic and paradox, furnished the most powerful philosophical stimuli. Much of this traditional heritage has been revived in the current dialogue with

Western philosophy. The Zen heritage has become Asia's gift to the universe of knowledge, a gift of lasting worth that also points to the future.

Three

RESEARCH ON ZEN

European research into Buddhism began in the nineteenth century. Following the Western lead, scholarly inquiry into Buddhism got underway in Asia at the beginning of the twentieth century, contemporaneous with a religious revival.[1] As recounted in our first chapter, research into Zen was initiated after its introduction in the West, and its enormous development is one of the defining features of Zen in the twentieth century. Here we can give only a very selective account of the most striking results of this research. Our survey begins with the linguistic questions, which are currently attracting great attention.

LANGUAGES AND TRANSLATIONS

Linguistic creativity has been a feature of all forms of Zen. Translation of the Buddhist schools into the language and culture of China was itself an immense achievement; a study of the emergence of Chinese Zen (Ch'an) shows how remarkably the Chinese movement differentiated itself from early Chinese Buddhism, which was closely tied to its Indian sources.[2] When did the *dhyāna*-masters become *ch'an*-masters? The novel element we meet in Ch'an first appears in the Taoistic features of sixth and seventh century literary testimonies. The language of the Ch'an literature is so different from the classical Chinese used by Confucian scholars that Ch'an was at first wholly opaque to early European sinologists. It has only gradually come to be understood. In our day, the Japanese scholar Iriya Yoshitaka has made great progress in research into the language of the Ch'an literature.[3] Relying on Iriya's linguistic works, his colleague and friend Yanagida Seizan made much-acclaimed contributions to historical research, radically transforming our notions of the development of the Ch'an tradition.

Of most linguistic interest in this literature are the collected sayings of the masters and the koan collections that draw on these, full of popular idioms and ambiguous expressions. The chronicles of the later T'ang period (618–907) and the Sung period (960–1279) contain much similar material in their lively but not always historically reliable biographical sketches. There are several English translations of the sayings of the greatest Chinese master, Lin-chi (d. 866).[4] The French translation by the scholar Paul Demiéville includes an excellent commentary.[5] The robust Chinese of the early masters abounds in the writings of Lin-chi's teacher Huang-po (d. 850), the original and profoundly humorous Chao-chou (778–898), and Ta-chu Hui-hai, whose master Ma-tsu (709–88) praised him as a "great pearl (Chinese: *ta-chu*), the perfect and bright luminance of which penetrates everywhere without hindrance."[6] Charm is added to these collections by the inclusion of koan-like episodes from the lives of the masters, taken from the chronicles.

The koan is, linguistically, a form unique in religious literature. The koan collections still used today in Zen halls, the *Mumonkan* and the *Hekiganroku*, have attracted great attention in the West. The first

Zen text translated into German was a koan anthology compiled and annotated by Zen master Ōhasama Shūei with the help of August Faust.[7] Wilhelm Gundert's (1880–1971) translation of the *Hekiganroku*, the most refined work of Chinese Zen literature, is a masterpiece of poetic empathy; unfortunately he completed the translation of only sixty-eight of the hundred cases, and after his death no one was able to continue the work at anything like the same level.[8] In English there are several complete translations of the collection.[9] The *Mumonkan*, a collection of forty-eight koans, less valuable but very popular among Japanese Zen masters, has been translated into German by the sinologist Walter Liebenthal, who vividly conveys a sense of the Chinese setting; my own version, based on the rich Japanese tradition of commentary, aims to combine fidelity with clarity.[10,11] Stimulating commentaries (Japanese: *teishō*) on the individual cases are given in the English translations by the Japanese Zen masters Shibayama Zenkei (1894–1974) and Yamada Kōun (1907–89), based on oral instructions given to encourage practitioners during a *sesshin*.[12]

Japanese Zen literature—original Japanese work that does not merely comment on Chinese sources—is not held in as high regard in Japan as is the Chinese literature; the original sources of Zen, especially the great masters of the T'ang period, are thought to enjoy an unattainable superiority. Yet in reality the quality of the Japanese work is only slightly inferior. It presents its own linguistic difficulties due to the profound alterations the Japanese language has undergone through the centuries. Japanese and Western scholars have spared no pains to unlock the philosophy of these texts. In the last decades a Japanese collection of twenty volumes has been published, combining well-introduced and extensively annotated sayings and writings of Japanese Zen masters with translations into modern

71

Japanese.[13] Western researchers have drawn from this treasure, and many important texts have recently been made available in translation.

After Myōan Eisai (1141–1215), who brought the Lin-chi line that flourished in the Sung period from China to Japan, the most prominent Rinzai masters—many of whose writings are now available in English—are Bassui Tokushō (1327–87), Ikkyū Sōjun (1394–1481), Musō Soseki (1275–1351), Takuan Sōhō (1573–1645), Shidō Mu'nan (1603–76), Bankei Yōtaku (1622–93), and Hakuin Ekaku (1685–1768).[14–20] There are good editions in Japanese of the collected works, or at least the principal works, of these masters.[21] The Ōbaku school, the third Japanese Zen school along with Rinzai and Sōtō, was introduced into Japan by Chinese Rinzai masters near the end of the Ming period (1138–1644). The school's teaching methods and life-style show the Chinese influence of its founder Yin-yüan Lung-chi (Japanese: Ingen Ryūki, 1592–1673). Its first Japanese representative was the monk Tetsugen Dōkō (1630–82), who made his name by printing the Buddhist canon (*Tripitaka*). His chief writing is a set of doctrinal speeches in pure Japanese *kana hōgō*, named after the Japanese syllabic script *kana*. The young Swiss scholar Dieter Schwaller has provided a German translation and a thorough study.[22] The *kana* style of the Tokugawa period has its own philologically interesting linguistic form.

The linguistic accomplishments of Dōgen have been discussed in the previous chapter in connection with his philosophical insights.[23] His experience, originating in the decisive illumination he received in China when practicing under Master Ju-ching (1163–1228), unfolded in linguistic creations that can in turn be understood only in light of that experience. His own way to enlightenment carries a Chinese stamp, as with so many Japanese masters, and this too has its linguistic aspect. His first writing on his return to Japan (1227) was written in Chinese characters (*kambun*): *Fukan Zazengi* (*General Teachings for Encouraging Zazen*), a protreptic for the zealous pursuit of Zen, includes a precise description of sitting erect in meditation.[24] Dōgen's collection of three hundred koans in Chinese is also still in existence. It probably served as the basis for his numerous talks, along with the so-called *Kambun Shōbōgenzō*, which is no longer extant. He successfully converted into Japanese what he had learned in China, producing a language that differs not only from modern Japanese but from the speech of his time. He loves to cite from the Chinese Zen literature as the starting point of his reflections or as confirmation of his insights. His language is obscure above all because he brings into the Japanese vernacular Chinese idioms of the Sung period that are only now being discovered by Japanese philologists. Thus the ninety-two books of the *Shōbōgenzō* set difficult tasks for linguistic scholarship, which will continue to challenge researchers in Japan and the West.[25]

The satisfactory translation of Dōgen is a task that has not yet been completed. The Nishiyama/Stevens translation is more than a paraphrase, but while it can give an introduction to Dōgen's thought, it would be unfair to make rigorous scholarly demands.[26] Of more value are the excellent translations of key chapters that have appeared in *The Eastern Buddhist*.[27] Books and articles on Dōgen sometimes contain extensive and reliable citations from his work. The Western reader who has some acquaintance with Japanese will find assistance in the well-annotated versions in modern Japanese, but these must be used discerningly, for in these translations the difficult but important passages in the text are often dealt with only vaguely. At present great progress is being made in translating Dōgen, and we can perhaps count on its satisfactory accomplishment by the end of the century. On the linguistic level, this translation is one of the great contributions of Zen research in this century.

TRANSFORMATIONS OF THE HISTORICAL PICTURE

Suzuki Daisetsu transmitted to the West the traditional view of Zen history. As a member of the Rinzai school, he saw the beginnings of Zen and its history in China in the light of his school. In the *Essays in Zen Buddhism* he recounts the Bodhidharma legend and the triumph of the southern school of the Sixth Patriarch Hui-neng in the style of the extant Ch'an writings, the *Platform Sutra* and the Sung chronicles.[28] Later he recognized that only a few of the writings of Bodhidharma were historically authentic. Historical research was foreign territory to Suzuki, as his famous controversy with his Chinese colleague Hu Shih dramatically revealed.[29] Many Western books have uncritically adopted his historical views.

Most accounts of the history of Chinese and Japanese religion treat the beginnings of Zen inadequately. Japanese Zen, introduced into the country during the Kamakura period (1185–1333), is presented as "the religion of the samurai"—a cliché that contains an element of truth but needs careful qualification.[30] The development of the Zen school during the later centuries is usually given only summary mention, and the history is rounded out by some modern-day statistics.

The awakening of interest in Zen by Suzuki and others in the middle of the century naturally made its history, too, a topic of study. The first translations of Zen literature aroused interest in Zen's fascinating personalities and their historical interconnection. It is as true of Zen as of anything else that its history reveals its meaning and essence and that it cannot be satisfactorily understood without knowledge of the major historical developments. During the last forty years scholars have identified the most salient historical questions and begun addressing them step by step.

The first task was to discover the movement's spiritual sources and its first leaders. Suzuki had done historians a service in emphasizing the important role of the Mahāyāna sutras. Japanese Zen scholars see Zen in the context of the manifold development of Mahāyāna Buddhism in East Asia. Western scholars, on the other hand, have been struck by the clear affinities with the philosophy of Taoism and have tended to see Zen as a Buddhist variant of the Taoist tradition. This view has proved untenable, for living Zen as practiced in Asia today leaves no room for doubt about its radically Buddhist nature, though there certainly has been a strong Taoist influence.

Bodhidharma and the Beginnings of Zen Justified doubts about the historicity of Bodhidharma, the founder of Ch'an in China, were raised at the beginning of the century. The extremely rich excavations of the Buddhist caves at Tun-huang, at the north end of the Silk Road, brought to light numerous manuscripts that altered and completed the picture of Chinese Buddhist history. The rediscovered Ch'an writings shook the Bodhidharma legend. The first shock to the learned world came from the eminent French orientalist, Paul Pelliot. In the description of a Chinese Buddhist temple composed by Yang Hsüan-chih in 547, Pelliot discovered the name of a monk, Bodhidharma, who had visited the Yung-ning temple, praised its beauty, and claimed to come from Persia and to be 150 years old.[31] Could this be the legendary Bodhidharma? Later Ch'an manuscripts aided in dismantling the legend as they revealed its gradual development and attested to the deviations from the Ch'an chronicle of the Sung period, *Keitoku Dentōroku* (1004).

Today the historicity of Bodhidharma, though not irrefutably proven, is generally accepted. The brief vita in the historical work of Tao-hsüan (d. 667), "Continuation of the Biographies of Famous

Monks," (Japanese: *Zoku-kōsōden*, composed 645, revised 666) is regarded as the most important source of information on his life and work.[32] This simple and restrained biography has some material that could have helped to create a legend. It describes Bodhidharma as a Brahman from South India, a Mahāyāna monk devoted to meditation, who came by sea to South China, traveled north, and met resistance as he spread his teaching of enlightenment. Tao-yü and Hui-k'o (487–593) are named as his disciples; Hui-k'o is usually numbered as the Second Patriarch. But it is significant for the history of Zen that Tao-hsüan does not present Bodhidharma as the founder of a school or the transmitter of a spiritual tradition. His wisdom and meditative absorption are praised, but there is no mention of a particular way of enlightenment. He mentions Bodhidharma's wall-meditation (Chinese: *pi-kuan*) but not the legend that he spent nine years gazing at a wall and that he was the twenty-eighth in a line of Indian patriarchs. The first we hear of a Chinese patriarchate and the succession of generations of patriarchs from Bodhidharma is in chronicles from the eighth century. With the demise of the Bodhidharma legend, the task of showing when and how the Ch'an meditation schools took form in China devolves upon historians.

The two and a half centuries after Bodhidharma and Hui-k'o, an important and eventful period in the development of Ch'an, remain imperfectly known despite intensive research. However, our present findings go far beyond what was believed fifty years ago on the basis of confident acceptance of the chronicles. There was some contradiction of this tradition by Suzuki and still more by Hu Shih. Yanagida Seizan, more than anyone else, has devoted long years to the study of the sources and sheds light on this dark period. His standard work, "Studies on the Writings of the Early History of the Zen School," complemented by numerous individual studies and monographs, has led to a decisive breakthrough in our knowledge of the period.[33] Yanagida's work has been extended by intensive Zen research in the West, especially in the United States.

In the traditional tables, which give a graphic image of the origins of Zen in China, the first five Patriarchs are Bodhidharma, Hui-k'o, Seng-ts'an, Tao-hsin (580–651), and Hung-jen (601–74). But here, too, historical verification is required, for the generational sequence that ensures the transmission of the doctrine is uncertain. The verse often cited as characteristic of Bodhidharma is first found as a fixed formula in the Sung period (1108):

A special transmission outside the writings,

independent of words and letters:

Directly pointing to the heart of the person—

to see (one's own) nature and become Buddha

A special difficulty attaches to Seng-ts'an, who serves as the connecting link between the first two bearers of the tradition, Bodhidharma and Hui-k'o, and the two abbots on the East Mountain, Tao-hsin and Hung-jen. We are given his name and the probable date of his death, but there is no smooth transition between the two phases of the early period. We have no factual information about the meditation methods of Bodhidharma and Hui-k'o.[34] Tao-hsüan's enigmatic remark about Bodhidharma's Mahāyānist gazing at a wall tells us little; even the writing attributed to Bodhidharma on the "Two Entrances and Four Practices," with the preface of T'an-lin, no doubt the oldest written document of the Bodhidharma tradition, does not discuss Bodhidharma's particular method of meditation.

East Mountain Ch'an The second phase of Ch'an is the "Dharmagate of the East Mountain," named after the residence of the Fifth Patriarch Hung-jen (601–674). Early accounts indicate a turn to the monastic, beginning in the time of the Fourth Patriarch Tao-hsin, whose monastery was located near the East Mountain. Many monks gathered around the Fourth and Fifth Patriarchs, shared their sedentary way of life, and gave Ch'an deep roots in Chinese soil. Information about their form of meditation appears in two of the Tun-huang manuscripts. *Records of the Masters and Disciples of the Lankāvatāra*, from the beginning of the eighth century, contains a lengthy text that is attributed to Tao-hsin and whose redaction is dated to 716 by Hu Shih and Yanagida.[35] This is not an authentic writing of Tao-hsin, but a later collection of sayings and commentaries on the theory and practice of meditation. Similarly, the second important text of East Mountain Ch'an, the *Treatise on the Essentials of Cultivating the Mind,* (Chinese: *Hsiu-hsin You Lun*; Japanese: *Shushin Yōron*), was compiled by Hung-jen's disciples about 720 and attributed to Hung-jen.[36] Both works present the East Mountain doctrine at the beginning of the eighth century; it is not clear which is of earlier origin. They give a clear picture of the spiritual situation before the split into the Northern and Southern schools of Ch'an.

The title of the Tao-hsin text, *Essential Teaching of the Expedient Means of Pacifying the Mind and Entering the Path,* (Chinese: *Ju-tao An-hsin Yao Fang-pien;* Japanese: *Nyūdō Anshin yō Hōben*), recalls the Bodhidharma tradition in which entry into the way, the Tao, is often invoked, signifying the complete experience of enlightenment. In its content the text is indebted to the Mahāyāna sutras and is close to the Tendai school. It teaches the "*samādhi* of one exercise" (Japanese: *ichigyō sammai*) already recommended in the *Wisdom Sutras*. The key is "maintaining the One without wavering," (Chinese: *shou-i pu-shun;* Japanese: *shui fui*); the Hung-jen text similarly insists on "guarding the mind," (Chinese: *shou-hsin;* Japanese: *shushin*). Attention to the One, namely the mind, is the precondition for any deep experience.

The last of the five gates of Tao-hsin is "Maintaining unity without going astray—dwelling at once in movement and rest, one can see the Buddha nature clearly and enter the gate of *samādhi*."[37]

The text does not provide a unified doctrine of Ch'an meditation. It quotes many Mahāyāna sutras and links various philosophical currents, such as Yogācāra and Mādhyamika. Even the invocation of the name (Japanese: *nembutsu*) has its place. In this multifaceted collection of meditational lore, later branches of the Zen lineage could easily find confirmation for their theses. Tao-hsin remains close to the Indian tradition of a gradual, step-by-step approach to meditation, but also often mentions the suddenness and spontaneity of the word. To the question of how the mind can attain the purity of enlightenment, he replies: "Do not practice mindfulness of the Buddha, do not grasp the mind, do not view the mind, do not meditate, do not contemplate, and do not disrupt the mind. Just let it flow. Do not make it go and do not make it stay."[38] He speaks of the sudden spontaneous lighting up of the Buddha-nature, the mind as a bright mirror discovering its own original purity, the Dharma-eye lighting up spontaneously. But he also teaches gradual progress to perfection through meditative practice. It is the master's business to lead the disciple along the path best suited for him.

In regard to Ch'an meditation we consider Tao-hsin and Hung-jen together, for scarcely any differences or transitions can be discerned between them. Hung-jen, according to early accounts, was a personality of great radiance. To him, more than anyone, the East Mountain movement of the Dharma-gate owes its role in early Ch'an history; this can at last be fully assessed in the historical studies based on the Tun-huang finds. After Tao-hsin's death, the East Mountain Ch'an community made its most profound contributions under Hung-jen's guidance. The treatise ascribed to Hung-jen emphasizes guarding the mind—the meditative task is steady concentration, keeping the presence of the mind in consciousness: ". . . maintaining awareness of the True Mind is superior to reflecting on Buddhas divorced from oneself."[39] Maintaining this awareness is the foundation of nirvana, the key to entry into the path, the basic principle of the Buddhist canon, the highest way, and the ultimate duty of the meditator. Hung-jen tirelessly drives this home to his disciples: "if one can just distinctly maintain [awareness of] the mind (shou-hsin) and not produce false thoughts, then the Dharma sun of nirvana will be naturally manifested."[40] This conviction is based on his faith in the original purity of the mind.

Like Tao-hsin, he uses the metaphors of sun and clouds, mirror and dust, which have a place in Chinese culture beyond Buddhism. Their parallelism is clear. Sun and mirror, by nature, shine as the originally pure mind; cloud and dust can tarnish them for a while but cannot injure their basic radiance. Hung-jen unites the two metaphors when he writes that "The Buddha-nature embodied within sentient beings is inherently pure, like a sun underlaid by clouds. By just distinctly maintaining awareness of the True Mind, the clouds of false thoughts will go away and the sun of wisdom will appear. . . All concepts, as well as the affairs of the three periods of time [should be understood according to] the metaphor of polishing a mirror: When the dust is gone the Nature naturally becomes manifest."[41] One might expect him to go on to urge the disciples to polish the mirror eagerly and remove even the smallest speck; such advice is found in other East Mountain texts, such as the *Records of the Masters and Disciples of the Lankāvatāra*: "It is also like the polishing of a bronze mirror: When the dust is completely gone from the surface of the mirror, the mirror is naturally bright and pure."[42] Another text of the school reads:

Although the [Pure] nature is without darkness, it is obstructed by the clouds of false thoughts. It is like the dust
on a bright mirror—how can it possibly damage the
[mirror's] essential brightness (*ming-hsing*, or "brightness
nature")? Although it may be temporarily obstructed, rub-
bing will return the brightness. The brightness [of the
mirror] is a fundamental brightness, not like something
appended to it. The Dharma nature is the same.[43]

Thus this aspect of the mirror metaphor was known in East Mountain
Ch'an, though, as McRae notes, "the reflective or illuminative capacity of the mirror is a fundamental characteristic that is not really
affected by the adventitious appearance of dust on the surface."[44] It
gave grounds for the claim made, in the confrontation between the
Northern and Southern schools, that the Northerners were devoted
to a gradual ascetic effort to polish the mirror, ultimately futile,
whereas the Southerners enjoyed sudden enlightenment in the discovery of the mind's original purity. However, careful study of the
East Mountain writings shows that they provide no basis for the later
controversial opposition of suddenness and gradualness in enlightenment.

East Mountain Ch'an as revealed in the texts attributed to the
Fourth and Fifth Patriarchs has an open, appealing character and "a
very gentle approach to spiritual practice."[45] Naturally, Tao-hsin
and Hung-jen urged their disciples to zealous practice, but their
methods of guidance were relatively mild. The disciples were to
concentrate on correct sitting, calming the mind, and above all
guarding the mind, avoiding all unnatural forcing. In any case,
success would depend on the individual's talents. When the end of
the Hung-jen text deals with the attainment of Buddhahood there is
no talk of the "suddenness" or "gradualness" of enlightenment, but

those who are earnest in meditation are urged to be convinced that they can attain emancipation: "Those who are listening [now] should make effort, so that you can achieve Buddhahood in the future. I now vow to help my followers to cross over [to the other shore of nirvana]."[46]

Finally, let us note that in the East Mountain texts we find the earliest practical Zen instructions, for example, in the Tao-hsin text: "When you are beginning to practice seated meditation and mind-viewing, you should sit alone in a single place. First, sit upright in correct posture, loosen your robe and your belt, and relax your body by massaging yourself seven or eight times. Force all the air out of your abdomen. . . . By regulating the body and mind one can pacify the mind . . . One's breathing becomes tranquil and the mind gradually regulated."[47] Such indications, which recur in various writings, are particularly precious since there were no proper manuals of Zen meditation until a later date.[48]

The Northern Ch'an School The so-called Northern school separated from the Southern school at the historically momentous Great Dharma Assembly (Japanese: *Daihō-e*) at the temple monastery Ta-yün-ssu (Japanese: *Daiunji*) on January 15, 732. The classic account of the proceedings, based on Southern sources, sums up the dispute in the slogans "Suddenness of the South" (Japanese: *nan-ton*) and "Gradualness of the North" (*hoku-zen*). It places the Northern school in an unfavorable light and names the Sixth Patriarch and founder of the Southern school as the second founder of Ch'an in China. A long-awaited revision of this account has been achieved by Western scholars following Yanagida, who have interpreted and assessed the Tun-huang writings from the Northern camp in a series of thorough studies.[49]

The term "Northern school" comes not from its adherents but from Shen-hui (684–758),[50] the militant disciple of Hui-neng (638–713), who raised the banner for his master at the Great Dharma Assembly and proclaimed him to be the Sixth Patriarch.[51] Several of the ten outstanding disciples of Hung-jen (the Fifth Patriarch) were leading figures in the East Mountain school and precursors or pioneers of the Northern school. The eldest disciple, Fa-ju (638–89), propagated the East Mountain style of Ch'an in Northern China, and his epitaph contains the earliest listing of the generational sequence of the first patriarchs, probably his own invention. The early chronicle of the Northern school, *Dembōhōki*, gives the first written listing of the sequence, which like other controversial issues was decided in the struggle for power in favor of the Southern school. The name of Fa-ju attracted little attention in later Zen historical works.

Shen-hsiu (606–706) was given the status of founder and leader of the Northern school in the historical picture shaped by the victorious Southern school, though he is judged to be a man of lesser quality (and of course denied the title Sixth Patriarch). This highly refined monk of aristocratic background is undoubtedly one of the outstanding personalities of Chinese Buddhism. After Hung-jen's death (674) the Ch'an center on the East Mountain lost much of its attraction, and Shen-hsiu oversaw the transition into a new phase. His biography affirms his standing as a Ch'an master; his successes in Lo-yang and Chang-an during the last years of his life assure him a place in the history of the Middle Kingdom; the pomp of his funeral testifies to his fame, recorded by the court poet Sung Chih-wen and in the posthumously granted title of "Dhyana Master of Great Penetration" (Chinese: *Ta-t'ung Ch'an Shih*).[52] After his death the mantle fell first on his fellow disciple Lao-an (also Hui-an, 584?–708), who was also highly esteemed at the Imperial Court and who was of great service to the school through his disciple Chih-ta (or Hui-ta), a prolific writer.[53] Lao-an died suddenly, and he was succeeded by another disciple of the Fifth Patriarch, Hsüan-tse (died before 727), who wrote about the masters and teaching of the *Lankāvatāra Sutra*; his disciple Ching-chüeh (683–c.750) integrated this writing, in part, into his *Records of the Masters and Disciples of the Lankāvatāra* (Japanese: *Ryōga Shijiki*; Chinese: *Leng-ch'ieh Shih-tzu Chi*).[54] Independently but simultaneously, the lay disciple Tu Fei composed what is undoubtedly the most important text of the Northern school, the *Dembōhōki* (Chinese: *Chü'an Fa-pao Chi*), presenting the school as mainstream Ch'an. The little it tells us about the transition from the East Mountain school to what has entered Ch'an history as the Northern school shows the latter's close connection to early traditions and the key role played in its formation by Hung-jen's disciples.

The next phase encompassed the controversy between North and South; it culminated in the Great Dharma Assembly of 732, which did not injure the Northern school as deeply as the Southern school claimed. Modern research persuasively documents the considerable activity of the Northern school during the first four decades of the eighth century. Chief among Shen-hsiu's disciples is P'u-chi (651–739).[55] Close connections with the court were also maintained by I-fu (661–731), who helped his master Shen-hsiu during the latter's final illness. We hear of a great number of other disciples of Shen-hsiu and of the throng of P'u-chi's disciples.[56] Grave inscriptions praise the merits of some particularly outstanding monks. The school was in its prime throughout the eighth century. At the Council of Lhasa (781), one of its adherents, Mo-ho-yen, represented the standpoint of sudden enlightenment.[57]

From this brief outline of recent findings, one can see that it is necessary to correct the received version of Ch'an history. The Northern school was far from ephemeral and without influence. Nor can the eventual decline of the school be attributed, as the Southern school suggested, to the attacks by Shen-hui and his disciples at the Assembly of 732. Rather, it may have been weakened spiritually by its close connections with the court. The ups and downs of Zen schools and branches are almost inevitable, given the lack of a central organization. In any case, we have one hundred twenty-five names of disciples in the lineage of Shen-hsiu as evidence of the vitality of the Northern school, which was active in China until the beginning of the tenth century.[58]

Within the school were proponents of both sudden and gradual enlightenment. The controversies about the generational sequence cannot yet be fully resolved, and many questions remain about the turbulent eighth century. From the turn of the ninth century, the *Platform Sutra* played a leading role. The two principal lines of Ma-tsu Tao-i (709–88) and Shih-t'ou Hsi-ch'ien (700–790) ushered in the golden age of Ch'an and determined its future path.

The Influence of the Northern School on Zen in Japan   Recent historical research on the Northern school of Ch'an has revealed its relationship to Japanese Zen. During the early period, the most important Buddhist center in Japan was situated on Mount Hiei near Kyoto, where the Tendai school imported from China had spun an elaborate web of teaching and praxis. Saichō (767–822), the founder of the Japanese Tendai school, had brought Zen from China in two lines, the so-called Northern school and the Ox-head school.[59] Earlier, Tao-hsüan (702–60), a Chinese disciple of the Northern school, had taught Zen meditation on Mount Hiei along with the rigorous Vinaya monastic discipline typical of his school. Yet for a long time, Zen played only a modest role in the center, which was so rich in meditation practices. This situation changed towards the end of the Heian period (793–1192). On this point, modern historical research significantly supplements the received picture.[60]

In the standard histories of Zen, Myōan Eisai (1141–1215) figures as the founder of the Japanese Rinzai school, which he brought to Japan after his second journey to China. Recently this account has undergone substantial modification. Modern research recognizes the special significance of one of the monks mentioned in the standard histories as Eisai's predecessors—Dainichi Nōnin (no dates available), the head of a so-called Japanese Daruma school. This school was close to Tendai Buddhism from the start, and Nōnin spent some time on Mount Hiei. With his disciples, he cultivated Zen-style meditation and revered the memory and writings (albeit apocryphal) of the Zen Patriarch Bodhidharma. A collection of writings of the Japanese Daruma school was recently discovered among the rich store of ancient material in Kanazawa Library (Kanazawa Bunko). Japanese scholars are now intensively studying these texts, which reveal un-mistakable connections with the Chinese Northern school. [61]

The headquarters of the Daruma school was the Sambōji monastery in Settsu. It had another seat in Tonomine, a Tendai center in Yamato that was destroyed in 1228. After Nōnin's death, his disciples scattered and one group settled in Echizen. These somewhat vague details have little importance in themselves, but what is important is the relationship that developed between the school and the great Japanese Zen master Dōgen (1200–1253).[62] The Daruma disciples who settled in Echizen were not far from the quiet, rural Temple of Eternal Peace (Eiheiji) that Dōgen, probably as a result of unhappy experiences in Kyoto, had set up as the headquarters of his school. Some of the Daruma school monks joined him and strengthened links that had been forged earlier by Dōgen's disciple and close friend Ejō, who became his successor. There is a paucity of precise information about Dōgen's relation to the Daruma school, but we can assume that its disciples carried the influences of the Chinese Northern school, which was a small stream feeding the mighty river of the Japanese Sōtō school.

Contemporary scholarly research on Zen has made its strongest impact in the historical field. The largely legendary historical picture of Zen has been substantially altered by critical historiography. Moreover, abundant new sources have been discovered, and we confidently look for further enlargement of our historical understanding. The new assessment of the Chinese Northern school is but one example of what has been achieved and what may be expected.

PSYCHOLOGY AND THERAPY

The reception of Zen in the West happened at a time in which Western psychology, through its new discoveries, had aroused uncommon general interest. The interplay of these two movements is one of the most fascinating aspects of twentieth century cultural history. Drawing on ancient traditions, the East was able to show Westerners new, unexamined paths into the psyche, culminating in the Zen path to enlightenment, the meeting point of old Indian Yoga experiences and Chinese Taoist spiritual heritage. Many Westerners were ready to join their Eastern counterparts in a common exploration of the *terra incognita*. It was in no small measure due to modern psychology that Oriental meditation spread so rapidly in the West. This conjunction was facilitated by D.T. Suzuki's openness to and understanding of modern psychology, which was still an avant garde movement when he first encountered it during his formative years in America. Though not everything Suzuki learned from James and others fitted easily into his Eastern outlook, his early experience with psychology was invaluable, especially in view of his continuing fruitful connection with Western psychology.

The Psychosomatic Totality of the Person The basic exercise of Zen, deriving from Yoga, activates the body very fully. This is a challenge to Western psychology which, focusing too narrowly on curing of illness, has long limited its concern with the body to the prevention and elimination of corporeally conditioned disturbances. Psychologists have also viewed Yoga and Zen chiefly in a therapeutic perspective; the ascesis of a yogi has been examined as a treatment for sickness.[63] This typical Western misunderstanding blocks access to the authentic character of Eastern meditation, which is always concerned with the salvation of the entire (physical and mental) person and knows nothing of the dualism of body and soul that stems from Greek philosophy. In the Asian outlook there is no separate body; the human being is at once body and soul, with the bodily and the mental united in a whole.

The basic exercise of Zen involves sitting in the lotus position and breathing correctly, both carried out not as medical measures but as basic conditions for meditation that put the person on the way to becoming self.[64] In the full-lotus position, the most perfect of the yogic ways of sitting (*asana*), the practitioner establishes an equilibrium of body and mind centered on the *hara* (literally, "belly"), the "earth-center of the person," in the words of the German psychotherapist and meditation master Count Dürckheim, who lauds the physical and mental benefits of "sitting in the *hara*." "Correct sitting is more than a condition for health and energy for work. Like all forms of bodily existence, sitting has a significance for every level of human life. . . . Sitting is in a sense the most basic exercise of all, the original home of the practice of stillness. . . . For it brings about a renewal proceeding from the roots of one's being, and all the more surely to the degree that one can empty one's mind of thoughts and images and sit with single-minded attention."[65] Zazen in the lotus position, carried out for several hours each day during a *sesshin*, is correct sitting *par excellence*.

Breathing is the fundamental vital activity of humans, and correct breathing, also derived from Yoga, is basic to Zen. While Yoga teaches many kinds of breathing, some of them quite complicated, Zen allows practitioners to regulate their normal breathing in slow and rhythmical inhaling and exhaling, through which the body is brought into a state of harmonious equilibrium. This is in accord with the oldest Buddhist tradition. The *Mahāsatipatthāna-sutta* in the Pali Canon describes the attentive breathing of a monk sitting erect in meditation at the foot of a tree: "Mindful he breathes in, and mindful he breathes out. Breathing in long, he knows, 'I breathe in long'; breathing out long, he knows, 'I breathe out long.'"[66] Zen practice usually begins with instructions from the master or his assistant on how to breathe correctly—slow, rhythmical breathing from the belly, first performed consciously, and later unconsciously. There is no form of Eastern meditation without correct sitting and correct breathing, the two physical preconditions for higher mental states. The basic exercise of Zen is thus a psychosomatic accomplishment in which the bodily is indissolubly linked with the mental.

Modern psychology has precisely demonstrated this coordination through investigation of the changes occurring in the practitioner's brain during the course of the exercise. Four kinds of brainwaves have been distinguished, each connected with and indicative of a particular psychical attitude.[67] The most frequently registered beta waves arise in the brain of the active person directed to the outside world; alpha waves accompany inner quiet and serenity; theta waves indicate a sleepy, twilight state of consciousness; delta waves correspond to completely unconscious sleep. These waves are measurable as electric potentials: variations of tension registered by

89

electrodes, magnified a millionfold by appropriate instruments, and recorded in the electroencephalogram (EEG) image as the transformations of consciousness. This technique was first used by psychologists for therapeutic purposes and later applied to Zen meditation. Experiments were successfully conducted in laboratories at Tokyo University and the Zen Buddhist Komazawa University, with Zen masters, Zen beginners, and contemplative Christian monks as subjects. The electrodes can be applied to the back of the head without damage to the skin. As expected, the Zen masters produced splendid, extended alpha waves, whereas in the case of the beginners the flow of alpha waves was often interrupted by beta waves. One astonishing finding was that after long sitting, the masters' alpha waves changed into theta waves, a sign that clear consciousness was being left behind. The Christian monks also produced alpha waves. These are associated with all contemplative, calm states and are disturbed by excitement and visible images.

The laboratory experiments also yield information about the kind of concentration attained during meditation. In one interesting experiment, the so-called click test, the meditator is roused from his state of recollection by a tone. The Zen masters registered the tone clearly, but after a momentary interruption the flow of alpha waves continued. In the case of the beginners, however, the waves were blocked for a considerable period of time. This experiment shows that the power of perception is not suspended in Zen meditation; the master sees and hears as clearly as a child, in clear contrast to the states of hypnotic insensibility produced by Yoga.

In biofeedback, the brainwaves produced during meditation activate a tone or a light so that the practitioner can compare his psychic state with his bodily changes. In an unfortunate reversal, one may attempt to produce the brainwaves in order to induce meditative states of consciousness and a transformation of consciousness. Japanese Zen masters have shown no liking for such procedures, just as they reject the use of hallucinogenic drugs; their interest in the results of research into the brain remains purely scientific and theoretical. Experimenters with other intentions gain no entry into Zen Buddhist monasteries and meditation halls.

The chief significance of the scientific psychological examination of Zen meditation is that it reveals with methodic precision the psychosomatic totality of the person. By integrating the body into meditation, and indeed giving it a foremost place, Zen permits experiments that show, precisely and graphically, the relation between bodily processes and psychic operations. But there is no basis for calling Zen masters "technicians of mysticism," as a well-known Western theologian has done. Zen masters are concerned with the spiritual needs of the practitioner and are well aware that "there is something in man that escapes all attempts at delineation and can never be measured by human methodology. . . . We can never equate the attainment of wisdom or the actualization of one's Buddha nature or union with God with any empirical evidence that can be measured by man or machine or the most delicate computer."[68] Here we run into the limits of scientific psychology.

States of Consciousness and the Unconscious   During the twentieth century, psychology has assumed an increasingly important place in cultural life, going far beyond its professional sphere. This is most evident in the influence exerted by Sigmund Freud (1856– 1939) and his early disciple and later rival Carl G. Jung (1875–1961). Jung was the first Western psychologist to discuss Zen extensively. His foreword to D.T. Suzuki's *An Introduction to Zen Buddhism* brought the Zen path into psychological perspective.[69] Suzuki had a special interest in the psychology of Zen. In an early essay he had expanded William James' well-known characteristics of mystical states of mind (ineffability, noetic quality, transiency, and passivity) to eight characteristics of satori: irrationality, intuitive insight, authoritativeness, affirmation, sense of the beyond, impersonal tone, feeling of exaltation, and momentariness.[70] This essay remains within the then-current framework of the psychology of mysticism. More important to Suzuki were James's frequent references to the transmarginal or subliminal forces of the subconscious and the significance for the religious life that he ascribed to them. James believed that this subliminal realm accounted for the greater part of the human essence. The subliminal realm was already well-attested, and James took up the call of a contemporary, Fredric Meyers, who had encouraged investigation of the entire spectrum of subliminal awareness.

One should note that the unconscious was not discovered by modern Western psychology but had been accepted in Asia since the first millennium B.C. The Indians observed attentively the various states of consciousness. In the *Upanishads*, in addition to the three states of waking, dreaming, and sleeping, there is a fourth state called *turiya*, "which is cognitive neither outwardly nor inwardly, nor the two together, nor is undifferentiated cognition, nor knowing, nor unknowing, which is invisible, ineffable, intangible, indefinable, inconceivable, not designable, whose essence is the experience of its own self, which is beyond diversity, which is tranquil, benign, without a second."[71] In the Buddhist doctrine of consciousness (*vijñānavāda*) the eighth consciousness is the "storehouse-consciousness" (*ālaya-vijñāna*; Japanese: *arayashiki*), also called *mumotsushiki* in Japanese (literally, consciousness sunk into nothingness); this can be interpreted as the unconscious or as a cosmic consciousness.[72] It is frequently invoked by Japanese Zen masters in clarifying the process of enlightenment. In the West, the influence of German Romanticism stimulated theorizing about the unconscious, prompting such views as that of C.G. Carus in 1846: "The key to knowledge of the essence of the conscious life of the soul lies in the region of what is unconscious."[73]

The encounter between Zen and Western psychology was facilitated by Suzuki's readiness to see satori as insight into the unconscious. Jung, echoing James' remarks on the limits of the field of human consciousness, elaborated in his own terms: "The world of consciousness is inevitably a world full of restrictions, of walls blocking the way. It is of necessity always one-sided, resulting from the essence of consciousness. No consciousness can harbor more than a very small number of simultaneous conceptions." In contrast, Jung continues, the unconscious or subconsciousness is of immeasurable breadth: "The unconsciousness is an unglimpseable completeness of all subliminal psychic factors, a 'total exhibition' of potential nature. It constitutes the entire disposition from which consciousness takes fragments from time to time." Zen allows "unconscious contents to break through to the conscious."[74] When Zen enlightenment is achieved, the entirety of the human psyche, with its conscious and unconscious contents, comes to light.

This is a purely psychic process: "The imagination itself is a psychic occurrence, and therefore whether an 'enlightenment' is called 'real' or 'imaginary' is quite immaterial."[75] Zen Buddhists would hardly agree with this last statement, for as Erich Fromm remarks in rejecting Jung's "relativistic position with regard to the 'truth' of religious experience," "it is of critical importance for them to differentiate between genuine *satori* experience, in which the acquisition of a new viewpoint is real, and hence true, and a pseudo-experience which can be of a hysterical or psychotic nature."[76]

Fromm was speaking at the conference on Zen Buddhism and psychoanalysis held at the school of medicine at the State University of Mexico in August 1957, in which D.T. Suzuki participated. As a proponent of a humanistic psychoanalysis, Fromm rejects Freud's libido-fixated image of human nature, nor does he confine the method to the treatment of sick people. The goal, in his view, is to break through logical, conscious thinking, which comprises only a small, insignificant part of the human psyche, in order to discover the unconscious, which is not merely Freud's dark cellar full of shameful disorders but also a source of creative powers and highest wisdom. Healthy persons, who enjoy a wholesome state of openness and alertness and whose existence is in accord with their human nature, have brought their unconscious over into consciousness, lifted all repression, and overcome anxiety and alienation. They are in touch with reality through their unconscious, which is an essential part of the whole person. Admittedly there are different levels in the unconscious, not all of which can be conquered simultaneously and in the same way.

In Fromm's view psychoanalysis has the same goals as those that Suzuki ascribes to Zen: "Zen in its essence is the art of seeing into the nature of one's being, and it points the way from bondage to freedom. . . . We can say that Zen liberates all the energies properly and naturally stored in each of us . . . to save us from going crazy or being crippled . . . giving free play to all the creative and benevolent impulses inherently lying in our hearts."[77] Both Zen and psychoanalysis are concerned with "the full awakening to reality . . . the undistorted and noncerebral perception of reality."[78] Fromm notes that Zen and psychoanalysis also share an ethical character, often overlooked in both cases. The ethical aspect of Zen is rooted in its living and effective Buddhist heritage, which demands above all the elimination of hatred and greed. "It would be a fundamental error to believe that the goal of Zen can be separated from the aim of overcoming greed, self-glorification, and folly, or that satori can be achieved without achieving humility, love, and compassion." Humanistic psychoanalysis, influenced by Jewish and Christian ethical values, is also "indissolubly connected with a change in character."[79] Despite the affinities between the goals of Zen and psychoanalysis, their methods and processes are radically different. Yet Fromm argues that koan practice and free association have a similar effect, that of driving the practitioner or the analysand into a corner, creating a situation of pressure that forces a breakthrough. The resulting non-rational, indefinable, sudden experience induces a transformation of consciousness.

This view of psychoanalysis goes beyond the usual empirical-psychological account in that it envisages a new, ethically-based realism that fully opens up the unconscious and that encompasses the feelings of the person. If repression is successfully lifted, "he will experience the futility of seeking the answer to life by *having* himself, rather than by being and becoming himself."[80] This metaphysical contrast of having and being is the summit of Fromm's philosophically inspired psychology. In his concluding remarks, he emphasizes that Zen is not a mere technique; it has its own set of ethical values and its roots are deeply embedded in the Buddhist monasteries where it developed. The metaphysical orientation of Fromm's psychoanalysis is not alien to Zen, as is clear when Suzuki counts a "sense of the beyond" among the characteristics of enlightenment: "The individual shell in which my personality is so solidly encased explodes at the moment of satori. Not, necessarily, that I get unified with a being greater than myself or absorbed in it, but that my individuality, which I found rigidly held together and definitely kept separate from other individual existences, becomes loosened somehow from its tightening grip and melts away into something indescribable, something which is of a quite different order from what I am accustomed to."[81] Here Suzuki echoes his mentor James: "the further limits of our being plunge . . . into an altogether other dimension of existence from the sensible and merely 'understandable' world."[82]

Therapeutic Effects of Zen Meditation Different kinds of Yoga accentuate different powers and functions of body and mind as they work together integrally in meditation. Hatha Yoga primarily activates the body, while Jhana Yoga and Bhakti Yoga appeal to the intellectual and emotional powers of the mind. Each Yoga exercise has a beneficial effect on the whole person. In Zen the basic exercise of sitting in the lotus position and breathing correctly focuses directly on the body with a corresponding psychic effect, involving the complete psychosomatic entity of the person. The mutual interaction of body and mind is verified by brainwave patterns: the peacefully flowing, expansive alpha waves attest to health and harmony of spirit. Other bodily functions can also be measured precisely—blood pressure, heartbeat, epidermal resistance—and they also reveal the beneficial effects on the organism. The slow rhythmic breathing also indicates the normal, healthy state of the meditator. Suitable nourishment and dress fill out the image of meditative practice in its outer, bodily aspect.

In due time the basic Zen exercise leads to certain mental accomplishments, resulting in powers of healing that are not directed toward any specific medical condition but all the more freely and deeply pervade the meditator's entire constitution. Silence is the first of these accomplishments. Zen is essentially silent meditation, and its silence embraces the whole person, cleansing and liberating, purifying and strengthening. During a deep silence that lasts for several hours, there emerges from the unconscious, as in psychoanalytical sessions, memories, representations, hypnotic images, and dream objects. These hours of silence are packed with inner events, until the desired stillness is attained. As in successful psychoanalysis, repressions are lifted, traumas are removed, anxieties are overcome. The therapeutic effect of silence is discreet and concealed, but penetrating and satisfying.

Zen meditation also brings into play another powerful inner process stemming from the contradictory attitude of the meditator toward the attainment of the enlightenment experience. He knows that the goal of his efforts is to experience enlightenment, yet he should in no way strive consciously towards this goal. Instead he must give himself passively to meditation in complete detachment, only following the direction of his master. Psychologists see in this paradoxical attitude the operation of "passive energy." The detachment that is demanded and practiced contains a power of healing that reaches the whole person. We see here why Zen insists on the absolute necessity of guidance by a master. The meditator can slip all too easily from the right track, either through an active and willful attempt to force success in the process of meditation, or through discouragement because of his failure to produce results.

Zen meditation can be of therapeutic value both to the healthy and to those afflicted with bodily or mental ailments. No one is so healthy that his or her psychosomatic condition is completely undamaged. But it must be clearly stated that Zen meditation is not a therapy for the mentally ill. One can perhaps go a step further and say that the Zen way, at least in its higher stages, is not suitable for all. Bodily posture, breathing, and silence may be recommended without reserve to everyone, and meditation certainly has healing properties of universal value. But certain features, such as the koan, should be used with discretion. As an experienced spiritual guide put it, "Gymnastics is good for everyone—acrobatics for a few," a remark as true in the mental realm as in the physical. It certainly applies to the superhuman rigor that the early Ch'an masters professed. Such acrobatic Zen is less frequently pursued today. The dilution of the demands of Zen has meant that what once could be reached only by a few in long practice and with extreme effort is now readily available to a large audience. This Zen-for-all may have much that is of value. In any case it is quite harmless and for many people represents a help along life's path. For the future of Zen meditation, a system of distinctions and gradations could serve as a guarantee of authenticity and effectiveness.

William Johnston remarks that the entry into deeper states of consciousness through meditative techniques cannot suffice for complete inner healing. He emphasizes that "love is the great healer,"[83] and names as a second indispensable healing factor the internalization of meaning. Love and meaning reach beyond the technical psychological realm, but both are at home in the religious sphere. These forces of healing are at work in religious meditation, Buddhist as well as Christian. We shall have more to say about this in the last chapter of this book.

The Morita Therapy The Japanese doctor Morita Masatake Shōma (1874–1938) completed his medical studies at Tokyo University and went on to study Western psychotherapy. Through various trials and experiments he invented and introduced into psychiatric praxis a new therapeutic procedure for psychogenic neuroses—the Morita therapy. The date given is 1919. Morita expressly insists that his method derives from Western medicine, yet it has unmistakable traits that point to Far Eastern, especially Zen Buddhist, influence. Both elements are found in Morita's warning not to overestimate the sciences and not to lose one's fundamental human understanding.[84] As a scientist he felt obliged to the West, and as a doctor he could Not deny his own healthy common sense. He created his unique method of treatment by combining his scientific knowledge, his religious and philosophical understanding of the world, and his practical experiences.

Born in Shikoku, the island of the great pilgrimage of Shingon Buddhism, and reared in the milieu of this religion, Morita's world view was shaped by Buddhism. During his decisive student years he took an interest in Zen Buddhism and several times took part in Zen courses under the guidance of the famous Zen master Shaku Sōen (1859–1919), practicing a koan. But he gave up these Zen efforts after some time. In later years he used his knowledge of Zen to add spice to his lectures and conversation.

The controversy about the degree of Zen mixed into the Morita therapy is still unresolved.[85] To doctors steeped in the Western scientific mentality, "Morita therapy is religion." Morita defended himself against this charge, pointing out that he sought to cure the symptoms of his patients not with philosophical or religious words but through an effective, concrete treatment. Yet he kept a certain distance from science, believing that there were all too many scientifically trained doctors who "clung to the motto 'illness, therefore medicaments'" and were "medically superstitious." "We should not forget that when science is overestimated and sound common sense lost the danger arises that the advantages of civilization will destroy humanity—a saying that seems prophetic today."[86]

Morita denied that his method derived from Zen, but he recognized correspondences with Zen, which some of his students later brought into clear prominence. His first student, Usa Genyū (1886–1957), was a Zen monk who turned to medicine at a late age and

99

studied under Morita from 1915 to 1919 at Tokyo's Jirei University, appropriating his teacher's newly developed methods. After completing his studies he became a monk at Tofukuji, one of the "five Zen mountains" of Kyoto. The temple put a piece of land at his disposal; there, in 1922, he built the first hospital entirely dedicated to Morita therapy. He directed his hospital, the Sanseiin, until shortly before his death and was succeeded by his son, Usa Shin'ichi, also a qualified doctor and an expert on Morita therapy.

Bruno Rhyner describes the Sanseiin's therapeutic methods, which he was able to understand in every detail with the help of Dr. Usa Shin'ichi.[87] During the first period, which usually lasts five to seven days, sometimes eight, the patient is absolutely confined to bed and is left entirely to his psychic situation. No speaking, reading, writing, listening to the radio, smoking, singing, whistling, or manual activity is allowed. Noises and thoughts come and go: the patient is not to worry about them. So he lies, hour by hour, day by day, sometimes sleeping at night and sometimes not. During this period of the "method of reduction," the patient is reduced in every aspect. The doctor visits him briefly once a day in order to keep track of his condition. This period is of special interest from the Zen point of view, in that the patient, as a result of his isolation, feels himself to be totally thrown back on himself, on his psychic condition and its symptoms, and this can produce a rather koan-like state of crisis, sometimes amounting to despair. Usually this state reaches its climax on the fourth day, and then suddenly turns into a state of rest, which is expressed in boredom and a desire to be busy. "Morita himself has called this psychical situation in which despair passes over into rest, or better, in which despair is identical with rest, 'the conflict is the solution' (*hammon soku gedatsu*)."[88]

The second three-day period brings the patient out of confinement into the open air. During this time he must stay in the garden as much as possible, even in rainy weather, indulging in only a few occupations but carefully observing nature and her processes. After the long stay in bed, this exposure to the open is refreshing and relaxing. The nearness to nature arouses the sleeping vital powers and revives the spirit.

The third period lasts about twenty days. Now the emphasis is on regular work. Inserted into the community of the hospital, the patient takes part fully in the common labor, delighting in it after his long inaction even when it is hard and tiring. He becomes one with the work, forgetting not only his sickness, its symptoms, and the effort he is making, but his very self. When this is achieved, recovery is near. Neurosis consists of states of anxiety or similar symptoms that totally occupy the patient's attention so that the anxiety increases further and requires even more attention. Fixation on the symptoms traps the patient in the diabolical round of what is medically called "psychic interaction." Healing can come only through a change in the direction of the patient's attention, and this is achieved by the work of the third period, which is not occupational therapy or a process of distraction but is intrinsically meaningful. This meaning is experienced by the patient as he devotes himself to the work with his companions. Feelings of depression and anxiety may recur, but now that he has embraced his condition they no longer hinder him from making his full contribution to the work, like everyone else. His entire attention is directed to the work assigned to him. There is a clear similarity between the second and third periods of therapy and the life and exercise of a Zen monastery. Whether this was deliberate or whether it stems from the natural sentiments of the country-born doctor cannot be determined. Nature and work are sources of strength for the healthy person, to the sick they provide harmless means of recovery. They fit into the Morita therapy in an unforced way.

The fourth period aims at reintegration into normal, everyday working life. The patient is given a great deal of freedom. He must leave the hospital at certain times, seek out his place of work and renew contact with his habitual environment. After about ten days he is considered cured and is released. The entire process has lasted about forty days. The cured patient remains in contact with the hospital through an aftercare group and attendance at the monthly lectures of the chief doctor.

The Morita therapy, an example of the encounter between Zen Buddhism and Western psychotherapy, has had statistically good results in Japan and has assured a place for itself without initiating any sweeping changes in theoretical and practical medicine. Its fusion of Eastern and Western science and experience, in a clearly delimited sector, merits study. The Eastern understanding of the human psyche, and especially of the psychosomatic totality of the human person, is superior to that of the West, which has for its part produced a global technology based on science. The cooperation of the two hemispheres promises great advances in the medical and psychological realm. During this century a comprehensive literature has been produced concerning the ancient therapeutic practices of India, China, and Tibet. Zen is but a drop in this ocean.

Four

ZEN MEDITATION IN CHRISTIAN PERSPECTIVE

When the World Parliament of Religions assembled in Chicago in 1893, the Far Eastern religions entered the West's field of vision, arousing admiration and expectations. It took decades for the effects of this encounter to become visible. A stimulus had been given, a process begun, and it was felt, especially in the religious milieu, that Asia would once again assist humanity on its spiritual way. Increasing contact with Asian countries, especially India, China, and Japan, seemed to confirm this.

During the first decades of the twentieth century, some new themes appeared at Christian missionary congresses, and these also had the effect of turning people's attention to the East. Louvain was the most important of the Catholic centers that had a strong impact on the renewal of missionary praxis. This praxis in turn prompted a look to the future. The colonial epoch was clearly coming to a close. Boldly prophetic thinkers recalled the cultural transformation achieved in the early Christian centuries. Had the time come to cast off the European mold? Could this contact with the East lead to another epochal breakthrough? Such thoughts created a positive atmosphere for the encounter between Buddhism and Christianity, which took place in a very specific form in Japan.

In February 1943 the German Jesuit Hugo Makibi Enomiya-Lassalle (1898–1990) took part in a Zen course in a country temple in southern Honshu. Knowing that neither lofty desires nor profound thoughts could substitute for personal experience and that Zen experience required more than a cursory acquaintance, Fr. Enomiya-Lassalle devoted himself to regular and strenuous Zen practice under a seasoned master. After more than twenty years of endeavor he felt he had sufficiently absorbed Zen to be able to communicate it to others. The student had now become a master. He began to teach in Germany in 1968, and his courses and evening lectures under the title "Zen Meditation for Christians" were immensely popular. This pioneer reached a wide circle, and other Zen courses for Christians were organized independently or were only loosely connected with his.

But after this initial breakthrough, the problems implicit in what is sometimes infelicitously called "Christian Zen" inevitably surfaced. Opposition based on little knowledge arose from the outside, while from within, intrinsic problems became apparent. Could Zen meditation, which had matured over centuries within Buddhism, be removed from its maternal soil and transplanted into Christendom without damage to one or both of the parties? This question was asked again and again in various forms by Buddhists and Christians, historians of religion, and instructors in meditation. Little satisfaction was found in the easy answer that only a method of meditation was being borrowed; Zen's very essence is shaped by Buddhist teaching, though Buddhist masters themselves recognize that it enshrines values that have a universal human core. The Christian encounter with Zen opens onto the wider tensions of the encounter of Buddhism and Christianity as well as of the Eastern and Western hemispheres. In what follows we shall examine this problem from various angles so that, even if we arrive at no completely satisfying solution, we will have the best possible grasp of the basic issues.

THE HUMAN QUALITY OF THE BASIC PRACTICE

The basic practice of Zen is zazen, that is, meditation while sitting in an erect position, in which the whole person is absorbed. The goal is to experience the real. Both the bodily and the mental are involved in this practice, which is an indivisible whole. But we can distinguish different components, some more concerned with the bodily and some with the mental, which strive together towards a higher state. In zazen the body is accorded a position of primacy. But in Eastern meditation the body is never seen as merely part of the person. When Zen Master Dōgen says, "Enlightenment is attained through the body," he sees in the body the enactment of zazen in its entirety as, according to his religious metaphysics, it manifests the identity of the human person with the Buddha-nature.[1]

Eastern meditation can be seen as centered on the rhythmical breathing that binds together the bodily and mental poles of the human being. This polarity is the chief feature of the underlying anthropology and is especially salient in zazen. A yogic exercise, in which breathing is linked to the basic movement of the human body upward and downward, invites comparison with zazen. The yogic practitioner standing upright in free space swings his loosely out-stretched arms downward past his knees, and then swings them upward. Meanwhile he attends to the regular rhythm of the breath, exhaling during the downward movement and inhaling during the upward movement. The text that describes the exercise concludes, "Above all the exhaling is important."[2] This exercise is not used in

Zen schools but can serve as an entry into the practice of zazen. The movement prepares the body for sitting in the lotus position. When the practitioner squats for zazen he must first bring the movement of the body into equilibrium. Traditional instructions for Zen meditation include letting the body swing in each of the four directions while focusing on one's breathing.

This conscious observation of one's breathing introduces a mental dimension into the exercise. The early Buddhist Satipatthāna meditation taught in the Pali Canon insists on attention (*sati*), which can be directed to physical or mental objects. As an aid to attention, Eastern meditation methods recommend the recitation of a word in tandem with one's breathing. The Christian spiritual guide Ignatius Loyola describes a form of prayer in which recitation of a word and rhythmical breathing are similarly conjoined. He describes this "third way of praying" as follows:

> Every time I breathe in, I should pray mentally, saying one word of the *Our Father* (or whatever prayer is being recited), so that only one word is uttered between each breath and the next. In the space between one breath and the next, I dwell particularly on the meaning of the word, or on the person addressed, or on my own worthlessness, or on the great difference between the magnificence of that person and my own worthlessness. The same regular scheme can be applied to the rest of the *Our Father*.[3]

The Eastern Orthodox Church also combines verbal repetition with regular breathing in the "Jesus Prayer" that the Russian pilgrim learned from the *Philokalia*. One utters at each breath the words: "Lord Jesus Christ have mercy on me!" The choice of words in these examples mark their specifically Christian character.

For the basic Zen practice, it is not essential to use a word of Buddhist stamp. Even without specific characterization by a word, the practice retains its validity. When words and phrases are absent or play a neutral role, one can speak of a secular meditation. Yet it would not be correct to say that in the basic Zen practice all religious references are cut off. The existential import of the practice itself entails a religious dimension, of which the practitioner is normally, though not necessarily, aware. When human beings perform this basic life function, breathing consciously, they gain insight into the texture of their existence and its fundamental religious orientation. In its Buddhist context, Zen meditation is religious in intention and accomplishment. This does not contradict its general human character, which allows diverse lines of development.

The universality of the basic Zen practice is due principally to its underlying conception of the polarity of human nature, which is enacted in breathing. Such an image of human existence is not unknown in the West, as Goethe's classic verses testify:

In breathing is a double good;
To take in air, to drop the load;
The first afflicts, the last relieves;
So strangely mixed is all that lives.
Then thank God when He sends you pain,
And thank Him when it goes again.

The poet associates a religious element with human and cosmic polarities and human wholeness. Within the specific religious tradition of Christianity the "theology of the heart" (*theologia cordis*) emphasized the unity of the intellectual and affective faculties, giving primacy to the heart as the principle of human wholeness. The Christian humanists who developed this theology insisted on the unity of mind and body and often stressed the importance of physical culture.

Romano Guardini stands out among those who have formed a Christian image of man in this century. Twenty or thirty years before

Zen arrived in the West, he drew on Far Eastern elements in the spiritual exercises that he conducted with students in Rothenfels Castle. A paragraph in his biography on the "discovery of the body" tells of the days spent at the castle in August 1924, during which one working group took up the theme of "gymnastics and rhythmics." When the young people found themselves in difficulties they called on their leader, and Guardini's contributions to the discussion were singularly illuminating. Rhythmics, he said, "has to do with the swinging of the body, a sensitivity to the cosmic, the cult of beauty," and gymnastics "relaxes the body in a way conducive to freedom, cheerfulness and health." He warns against allowing the rhythmic to become merely aesthetic. His attitude toward gymnastics is wholly appreciative. When the working group discussed which of the two pursuits was most valuable, he said: "We should practice gymnastics in a plain and simple fashion, but without being mistrustful of those to whom rhythmics means more; these in turn must respect the other's rights and not despise them as Philistines."[4]

A further step was taken with the well-attended spiritual exercises that Guardini first held in August 1930 at Rothenfels Castle and repeated in 1931 and 1932. He kept a record of the instructions, lectures, addresses, and meditations and published them in expanded form. In *Will and Truth*, one can detect something of the atmosphere this outstanding spiritual teacher created. Quiet, silence, concentration, restful recollection, solitude, presence, motivelessness—these words recur, reminiscent of the wisdom teachers of Asia. An orientation to wholeness is apparent from the start: "We are dealing with practice—not with thinking, but with doing. But thinking is involved, too, or rather, a living awareness in which intuition, inner experience and conceptual understanding become one." Thought and knowing are not excluded, but rather recover their appropriate place, embedded in the whole.

In his spiritual exercises, Guardini teaches object-directed meditation, regarding objectless meditation as proper to mysticism. When he gives practical advice on meditation, he presents silence and restful recollection as its primary conditions and describes it as an indivisible process: Meditation is "like the rhythm of a living whole: inhaling and exhaling, return to self and giving of self. The whole is what is called love. All the elements of 'practice' and 'technique' in meditation serve the sole purpose of releasing the sacred rhythm of love." Body-soul dualism is overcome. "The soul is spirit living in the body, referred to it, receiving from it, acting in and through it." The perspective of anthropological wholeness guides Guardini in the creation of his spiritual exercises, in which special stress is laid on gymnastics and breathing: " . . . breathing is a middle term through which the life of the body and that of the soul affect one another. When I exhale with a clear mind, in a mood of deep calm and cheer, it benefits the whole body and can clear away many discomforts. Conversely, a full and joyous breathing can free spirit and heart." Breathing also has cosmic import: "It is that rhythm whereby man stands in relation to the reaches of space, the sea, the air, the surrounding whole." Speaking and singing also have a place in his exercises, "not in connection with the 'soul' but with the living unity of the person, soul and body as a whole." Good speech and song become "a beneficial power, which inwardly touches and relaxes."[5]

The proximity between these spiritual exercises and the Zen way is clear from Guardini's use of the terms "relaxation," "growth," and especially "motivelessness." We have no precise information on his knowledge of Buddhism, but a striking passage in his book *The Lord* testifies to his encounter with the figure of the Buddha. He probably knew the Pāli Canon, at least in extracts, but not the *Meditation Sutra* (*Satipatthāna-sutta*), of which no trace can be found in his writings.[6]

His exercises precede the Western reception of Far Eastern meditation as a unique pioneering work.

In Western Christian spirituality, as the Japanese Carmelite Okumura Ichirō has noted, "the physical side of the mind and the spiritual side of the body have long been neglected."[7] Though this neglect is difficult to excuse, it is rooted in the soul-body dualism taught by classical Greek philosophy and sharpened by Gnostic and Manichean elements that played a leading role in the history of Western thought and extended its damaging influence to Christian spirituality as well. Although Christianity was preserved from metaphysical contempt for the body by its optimistic doctrine of being, the body was not accorded its full spiritual significance. Many Christians have become painfully aware of this lack as they register the growing threat that technology poses to body-spirit equilibrium. Under these circumstances, basic Zen practice offers itself as a remedy for the specific ills of modern society. In the West, the pressure and stress induced by the preeminence of technology and automation are now a matter of serious concern. An over-valuation of the rational for human progress, symptomatized in physical terms as a hypertrophy of the brain, which oppresses the rest of the body and damages the whole, has prompted a search for appropriate countermeasures. Christian spiritual leaders have found one in the way Zen integrates the body, or better, the bodily side of the spirit.

The basic practice aims at concentration. Thinking of and reciting a word on which all attention is focused, the practitioner seeks to clear the mind of all the thoughts and images that come up. In his early instruction encouraging the practice of zazen, Dōgen urges, "Throw all attachments from you, quieten the ten thousand things, think not of good and evil, judge not of correct and false, control the course of your consciousness, make the activity of wishing, representing, judging to cease." This is a difficult, drawn-out, painful endeavor, and immediate success is not to be expected. Before the mental eye of the practitioner, the world of images keeps arising, thoughts come and go, at times troubling hallucinations and visual apparitions arise; all sorts of disturbances upset the one who sits and strives for concentration. What is to be done? The Master says one is not to worry about what comes from the "devil's realm." But what is one to think about? Think of nothing at all, answers the Master. Dōgen concludes with the following practical counsel: "When a wish arises, note it, and when you have noted it let it go! As you practice a long time, you forget all attachments and come before yourself in concentration." This advice is entirely in the spirit of the early Buddhist meditation praxis, which seeks complete calming of the mind.

In a later version of the text, Dōgen adds a koan that leads further. The basic practice of Zen points beyond itself, maintaining a continual movement towards realization. The bodily side of the practice culminates in breathing and is aimed primarily at those who practice breathing while sitting erect, but it can go beyond this, in accord with its intrinsic cosmic dimension. The breath of the human microcosmos is linked to the cosmic breath of the universe. In Far Eastern thought the cosmos is grasped as a living whole, which breathes and lives by breathing. According to Zen Master Suzuki Shunryū (1905–71), "So when we practice zazen, all that exists is the movement of the breathing . . . our mind always follows our breathing. When we inhale, the air comes into the inner world. When we exhale, the air goes out to the outer world. The inner world is limitless, and the outer world is also limitless. We say 'inner world' or 'outer world', but actually there is just one world. In this limitless world, our throat is like a swinging door. The air comes in and goes out like someone passing through a swinging door."[8]

When Zen Buddhism and Christianity meet in the human element of the basic Zen practice, which includes an intrinsic religious dimension, they find themselves on common ground. Christian spirituality can be genuinely enriched by activation of the bodily, which Zen presents so convincingly and accessibly. Not the least of the reasons for Zen's strong appeal to the West is the relatively simple way in which it involves the body in meditative accomplishment. Such Eastern methods of integrating the physical, of which Zen is perhaps the most perfect, have after several decades won an established place in the West. Japanese Zen masters rejoice in this success of the meditation movement in Europe and America, to which they themselves have greatly contributed. And, as the best and most insightful of these masters have understood, the propagation of Zen elements has never found a soil better prepared or more favorable to a meaningful encounter than in Christianity.

WITHOUT THOUGHTS, WITHOUT IMAGES

The basic Zen practice on its mental side is directed to concentration. In deep, lasting concentration, the mind empties itself of all elements of thought, concepts, and images. The state of consciousness thus reached is known in Zen tradition as "without thoughts, without images" (Japanese: *munen musō*). In the koan exercises, too, this moment of transcending thought is very important.

When a Western visitor to a Zen monastery asks about the methods of meditation, the accompanying monk first tells him about sitting in the lotus position and about breathing. These explanations interest the visitor but do not entirely satisfy him. He asks further: "And on what does the practitioner meditate, when he squats in the lotus position? What does he think about?" "He meditates on nothing, he thinks of nothing," the monk answers with a smile. He sticks to his answer no matter how much the astonished visitor presses for further explanation. Zen meditation has no object; the practitioner does not meditate on any "something" but thinks, or at least tries to think, about nothing. Zazen is objectless meditation "without thoughts, without images."

Dōgen, the founder of the Japanese Sōtō school and the master of zazen, emphatically insists on this basic feature of Zen meditation. In his first writing, *General Teachings for the Promotion of Zazen* (*Fukanzazengi*), he urges: "Give up looking for explanations and chasing words! Learn to turn the light back on yourself and to let it shine on your own nature!" A few lines later he repeats the summons to stop thinking. He knew from his own experience that long practice achieves the forgetting of all objects. Dōgen had learned objectless meditation in China. His manual for the method shows the influence of a Chinese text of the Sung period (960–1279), the *Tso-ch'an i*, the earliest extant manual of zazen (composed about 1100), in which Master Ch'ang-lu Tsung-tse taught "forgetting objects."[9] In Japan, Dōgen's instructions were decisive for Zen praxis and were taken up by Keizan Jōkin (1268–1325), the Fourth Patriarch of the Sōtō school, in his *Memorandum Book for the Practice of Zazen* (*Zazenyōjinki*): "In zazen objects disappear of their own accord." This work was widely distributed and is still much used today.

The classic text for the definition of zazen as non-thinking freed from all objects is found in the koan-like dialogue, often cited by Dōgen, between a Chinese master of the T'ang period (618–907) and his disciple: "As the great master Yüeh-shan Hung-tao sat quietly, a monk asked him: 'Of what does one think while sitting?' The master replied: 'One thinks of not-thinking.' To this the monk replied: 'How does man think of not-thinking?' The master: 'Without thinking.'"[10] Dōgen finds in this conversation a satisfying expression of the essence of zazen. The unmoving bodily posture (in Japanese, *gotsu-gotchi* literally means "steep" or "towering alone") is the appropriate one for meditation. The ultimate not-thinking (Japanese: *hi-shiryō*) goes beyond thinking (Japanese: *shiryō*) and the preceding not-thinking (Japanese: *fu-shiryō*). The two negative expressions are scarcely distinguishable linguistically. The dialogue indicates that the way of zazen is a way of negation, which together with concentration in immobile squatting achieves enlightenment or already is enlightenment. In this objectless meditation one learns "not to touch things" and to see things as they are.

The objectless meditation of Zen is rooted in the metaphysics of Mahāyāna Buddhism, which through its focus on the "emptiness" of the world of becoming takes to its last consequences the early Buddhist teaching of non-self (Japanese: *muga*). Emptiness is the core concept of the Mahāyāna *Perfection of Wisdom Sutras*. The unfathomably deep wisdom sees through the emptiness of things. All things in the world of becoming are devoid of a proper nature; they are empty. This negative way, transferred to Zen praxis, signifies the forgetting of all objects and of the ego. As Klaus Riesenhuber writes in his landmark essay on objectless meditation, "Salvation lies in seeing through the 'emptiness' of the world of appearances and in the sublation this enables of the empirical, isolated ego into oneness with the breadth of the all, or, more deeply, with that which emerges as the basic underlying 'non-duality' (*advaita*) or 'nothingness' (*mu*) and thereby as the 'true essence', the 'original nature.'"[11]

The emptiness of the world of appearances, manifested in tireless negation in the Mahāyāna philosophy, provides the doctrinal foundation for the objectless meditation of Zen. If things are empty in their essence, they cannot stand as objects against a subject intent on apprehending their essence. The subject-object relation is unnecessary. The original mind "without thoughts, without images," free from the subject-object division, is called no-mind (*mushin*) in Zen. True reality is one. In the original unity there is no split, no separation, no duality. Master Suzuki Shunryū points out that non-duality finds its basis in the *Perfection of Wisdom Sutra*. He teaches his students that their practice, even if dualistic at the start, will acquire ever more unity.[12]

In the Zen Buddhist understanding of objectless meditation, the original Buddhist teaching of non-self comes into play. The practitioner, released from thinking and desiring, concepts and wishes, and from all clinging, becomes independent of things and forgets his empirical ego. This process needs no specifically Buddhist doctrinal content. As Riesenhuber explains:

> The objecthood of what one is aware of depends on the reflexive self- possession of the ego, which uses this world of distinct objects to assure its own unconditioned standing. Now if consciousness renounces this reliance on objects, in a gradual process of purification, then the ego— which as determined by reflection and reference to objects is different from the deeper True Self—abandons itself and sinks into the depth of the self or the mind which lie at a level prior to all subject-object division.

Thus emerges the possibility of a self or mind based wholly on experience, independent of "any objecthood or concrete content whatever."[13]

This objectless experience of self is an ontological experience, close to the experience of God, who dwells within us as creator. Riesenhuber's careful philosophical analysis establishes that in its essence and structure, objectless meditation is not tied to Buddhist doctrines. This does not alter the fact that Zen is based on Mahāyāna metaphysics and that it has never denied these origins. Yet it is possible to release the method of meditation "without thoughts or images" from the maternal soil of Buddhism and to see it as a fundamental self-realization of the human mind; when it is embedded in given religions and linked with their doctrines, objectless meditation will develop differently every time.

Objectless meditation is sometimes found among the Christian mystics who describe their paths of contemplation and immediate experience of God. They advise the beginner on the spiritual path to simplify his consideration of objects to a silent, loving gaze on the mystery of faith, on Christ as Savior, and on the heavenly Father, experienced as personally present. The ineffable reality of mystery and personhood transcends the plane of knowledge of objects. There is a progress on this path, as the mystics try to show by describing stages and degrees. Gregory of Nyssa, to whom seeing is not-seeing, appears familiar with an objectless meditation:

> As the mind proceeds even farther and more perfectly in
> true knowing, it will realize, the nearer it comes to vision
> . . . that the divine essence is invisible. When it leaves
> behind all that appears, not only what sense apprehends,
> but also what the mind seems to see, it constantly advances
> toward what is within, until with its striving it sinks in what
> cannot be seen or comprehended—there it sees God . . .
> and to see here means not to see.[14]

The Christian mystics describe the experience of contemplating the essence more fully than they do the way that leads to it, but they do describe stages of the transition from object-bound to objectless meditation. The "prayer of quiet," the lowest mystical stage, on which for the first time the object-related activity of the soul comes to a halt, probably corresponds to the *zammai* of Zen meditation, an absorption that is not yet complete enlightenment but preparatory for it.

Richard of Saint-Victor (d. 1173), who more than any other medieval teacher shed light on the operations and capacities of the human psyche in the mystical process, speaks of six stages leading to authentic mystical experience. The third and fourth of these surpass imagination, and the fifth and sixth surpass reasoning. What may be called the objectless meditation of the fourth stage deserves special notice in relation to Zen because of its focus on the self, for the enlightenment aimed at in the objectless meditation is often described as an experience of self and as the highest self-realization; in Mahāyāna the True Self is one with the Buddha-nature or absolute reality. At this stage, "leaving aside every service of the imagination, the mind directs itself to those things only which the imagination does not know, but which the intellect gathers from argument or comprehends through reason. . . . In this contemplation . . . our intelligence seems to grasp itself through itself." Then, "Let a person first learn to know his own invisible reality before undertaking to try to grasp the invisibility of God. The first thing is that you know the invisibility of your mind, before you can become capable of the knowledge of the invisible God." And finally, "From beholding the light that causes it to be inwardly amazed, the mind is enkindled and enabled to behold the light that is above it."[15]

Christians believe that in prayer and meditation the soul experiences consolations that come from divine grace. These could be compared with the Dharma-delight (Japanese: *hōetsu*) experienced in Zen practice. Ignatius Loyola accords great significance to the consolations in his *Spiritual Exercises* and explains their diverse causes and manners of operation. That which has the deepest effects, he teaches, is "spiritual comfort with no previous occasion giving rise to it." He explains: "'With no previous occasion' means without any preceding awareness of knowledge or anything which might induce such comfort in the soul, by means of its own acts of intellect and will." Such objectless consolation comes from God: "It is the Creator's prerogative to come into and leave the soul, to move it with inspirations of love for His Divine Majesty."[16] Explicators of the text speak of a mystical consolation. The practitioner who experiences this prays "without thoughts or images." His journals confirm that Ignatius was familiar with this manner of prayer. His spiritual exercises are open to objectless meditation and higher stages of spiritual experience.

These few examples show that objectless meditation has a place in Christian spirituality. This will be still clearer later when we compare Zen enlightenment with Christian experiences in light of negative theology. In its highest realization, objectless meditation touches the deepest level of the human spirit. It is perfectly possible, as Riesenhuber shows, to correlate this way of meditation with the Christian belief in revelation: "Objectless meditation, by reason of the fact that it cannot reflect on itself thetically, is open to discerning interpretation, indeed demands it, since absorption can only be a partial realization of human being, which has to understand itself reflexively in all its accomplishments." And he shows the possibility of a convergence of the two attitudes: "Surrender to the unconditioned mystery in the depth of the spirit does not take away from its revealedness in the person of Jesus, but is ordained towards this and makes it accessible to understanding (see John 6.45), as conversely historical revelation fortifies the meditative effort, insofar as the purpose of both is to lead to the depths of God under the guidance of the Spirit (see 1 Cor. 2.10)."[17] There is no reason to doubt that objectless meditation and Christian faith in revelation can be united and that their convergence can bear rich fruit.

The objections often made against the practice of objectless meditation, especially in Zen, are usually based less on questions of principle than on the supposition that such meditation leads inevitably to the neglect or even the relinquishment of indispensable Christian practices of piety. But these fears are baseless, as we shall see.

Let us look first at the expressions of Zen piety. Sutra recitation and ritual have long been part of the daily schedule of Zen monasteries. Western visitors to Zen temples, even historians of religion, have been astonished by the solemn ceremonies they have seen carried out by the abbots and their assistants. The Zen literature had told them of episodes in which a Buddha statue was burnt by a Zen master or a holy sutra by a disciple awakened to enlightenment. So they had imagined that in this school, which is independent of scriptural tradition, they would find no external religious observance. The sight of the Zen monks reciting the sutras daily before an image of the Buddha and celebrating elaborate rituals on such occasions as the taking of the Bodhisattva vows stands in stark contrast to common Western conceptions of Zen, as does the personal piety of Zen practitioners, seen in accounts of their experiences.[18] Finally, it should be remarked that the Japanese Zen schools repeatedly, over the centuries, successfully warded off the infiltration of the *nembutsu* (or invocation of the Buddha name), despite its popular appeal, and the magic rites of the Shingon school. It may be objected that these pious practices are not an integral part of the Zen way, since they are unmasked as "empty." This is correct, but let us note that according to the Zen worldview, based on the metaphysics of the Mahāyāna sutras, all external practices are provisional and the practitioner should cling to none.

Still less than Buddhists can Christians do without external gestures of piety. When they reflect on their practice, they see, as Riesenhuber said, that "absorption can only be a partial realization of human being" and that other basic forms of realization are indispensable. In practice this means that Christians cannot give up personal prayer and sacramental piety. Christian meditation leaders thus include the celebration of the Eucharist in the daily schedule. Experience shows that dedicated Christian students of Zen often develop a deeper personal prayer life and begin to read Scripture in a new way. To articulate the Christian character of the practice, many leaders give the practitioners a Christian key word for their path, or set up an image of Christ in the middle of the meditation hall. Such devices are not necessary, and there is some disagreement as to whether they are helpful or advisable. At this point, a plurality emerges within Zen meditation for Christians, and this plurality increasingly manifests itself in different respects.

In Christian tradition, objectless meditation is usually connected with mystical graces, but that does not mean that it cannot be used profitably by beginners on the spiritual path. Just this is what the successful practice of zazen by Christians seems to teach us. Many accounts relate how the radical emptying of consciousness in this meditation effects a profound inner purification, as if accumulated dust and unnecessary ballast were cleared away without a trace.

In Christian spirituality, objectless meditation cannot replace contemplation of objects, for the center of Christian prayer is the mystery of Christ and revelation. Zen meditation "without thoughts or images" does not usurp the place of Christian contemplation, which is dialogal, and leads to the higher stages at which the confrontation of subject and object issues in *unio mystica*. Yet the opposition to objectless meditation as such cannot be justified from a Christian standpoint. Christians and Buddhists are involved in similar behavior during objectless meditation, despite the different motivational contexts.

THE KOAN

In the Western reception of Zen, the koan has from the start attracted great attention. The precise function of this exercise remained unclear for a long time and has not yet been fully clarified. Westerners had difficulty in finding an intelligible meaning in the enigmatic, paradoxical exchanges between Zen masters and their disciples, in the utterances of ancient masters, in the episodes from Zen monastic life, and in the anecdotes of the early period. Daisetz T. Suzuki drew his readers' attention to the koan in the second of his three volumes of *Essays in Zen Buddhism* (1933). This was preceded by the first Western anthology of Zen texts, with a preface by Rudolf Otto, containing examples of koans from the representative collections *Hekiganroku* and *Mumonkan*.[19] Thus, from the start, the West saw Zen meditation as closely connected with the practice of koans.

This led to the discrediting of Zen by Western scholars of religion, as a result of its appropriation and misuse by various groups. Under the banner of Zen, American hippies of the sixties indulged in anarchic behavior; beatniks had delighted in the novel riddles of the koan. With the addition of drugs, the abuse reached a nadir that was never completely remedied. The popular work *Gödel, Escher, Bach* deliberately confuses the Greek philosopher Zeno of Elea and the Sixth Zen Patriarch Hui-neng, and, as a parody of the classic exchange between Achilles and the tortoise, invokes the famous koan in which the patriarch resolved the dispute between two monks as to whether the banner or the wind was moving: "It is not the wind that moves, it is not the banner that moves, the mind moves." Zeno finds in this koan the doctrine, "motion does not exist."[20] A well-known Dutch author of crime stories, Janwillem van de Wetering, who enriched his life with a stay at a Zen monastery, relates in his novel

The Empty Mirror and its sequel how, after he had struggled in vain with his koan for eighteen months, his master told him as he left that at the end of his path he would see "that enlightenment is a joke."[21]

Despite an extensive literature on the koan in Western languages, these misunderstandings have not yet been completely resolved. Koan (Chinese: *kung-an*) literally means "public notice or notification." Not much attention has been paid to this original sense. In fashionable Zen, the remarkable word was freely used for every sort of riddle or paradox, and it has now become a common term in the languages of several Western countries. Admittedly, the precise delineation of the complex connotation of the word is not easy, but we can trace the beginnings of the koan in the history of Zen Buddhism.[22]

The koan, as understood in Zen Buddhism, consciously or unconsciously includes a moment of questioning and doubt. The Zen practitioner is a seeker who turns for guidance and help to the master. The experienced, creative master is able to give the disciple the answer appropriate to him, which is imprinted indelibly on the questioner's memory. From this initial situation, we must suppose, the koan arose. The striking, terse answers of the masters were circulated widely among the disciples. The koan enjoyed greater esteem at the end of the T'ang period in the houses of Ummon and Rinzai, both distinguished by creative originality, serene humanity, and literary charm. Yün-men Wen-yen (Japanese: Ummon Bun'en, 864–949) is the Zen master who appears most frequently in the great collections. The community named after him was later absorbed by the Rinzai school, which assumed the foremost place in Sung China. Nan-yüan Hui-yung (d. 930), in the third generation after Lin-chi (Rinzai), was the first to use the sayings of earlier masters in the manner of a koan to lead people to enlightenment.

The koan is a Chinese invention and carries the typical mark of Chinese spirituality. Whereas Indians seek the essence of reality within and above things, the Chinese seek the deepest levels in the everyday. The history of the emergence of the koan in China testifies to the creative power of the old masters and their concrete method of teaching. Koan practice first flourished in Sung China, in which three figures of great, though diverse, quality stand out. Hsüeh-tou Ch'ung-hsien (980–1052), a master of the Ummon school and a poet of high rank, captured in verse the quintessence of the hundred koans in the *Hekiganroku*. Valuable commentaries were added a hundred years later by the notable Rinzai master Yüan-wu K'o-ch'in (1063–1135). The koans attained their widest circulation through his disciple Ta-hui Tsung-kao (1089–1163). At that time the Rinzai school articulated its dynamic character in opposition to the quietistic tendencies of the Sōtō school in the struggle between the "Zen of looking at the koan" (Japanese: *kanna-zen*) and the "Zen of silent enlightenment" (Japanese: *mokushi-zen*).

The popularity of koan exercises in the Sung period is not absolute proof of its efficacy for Zen purposes. The following generations were not able to equal the creative powers of the old masters in their use of the koan. Ruth Fuller Sasaki (1893–1967) names two causes of the decline of Zen in the Sung period: a falling off from the high level of creativity that the early masters had reached, and the excessive numbers of monks and lay students who flooded single temples in hundreds and even thousands in order to be instructed by especially esteemed masters.[23] The same development is described by D.T. Suzuki, and he sees the role of the koan as ambivalent: "Aristocratic Zen was now turned into a democratized, systematized, and, to a certain extent, mechanized Zen. No doubt it meant to that extent a deterioration; but without this innovation Zen might have died out a long time before. To my mind it was the technique of the koan exercise that saved Zen as a unique heritage of Far Eastern culture."[24]

It must be borne in mind that koan practice is merely a method, albeit one intimately connected with the essence of Zen and extremely efficacious. Ruth Fuller Sasaki explains that while the various schools of Zen developed different kinds of spiritual training, in all schools the chief path to the attainment of satori is the practice of meditation in the posture in which Shākyamuni the Buddha sat as he awoke to enlightenment.[25] Within the framework of meditation, the koan is a distinctive method that spread from the house of Rinzai to many branches of Zen Buddhism. The *Sōtō* school of Dōgen, a rival of the Rinzai school since both were introduced in Japan, does not reject koans; Dōgen himself was familiar with the koan during his period of study in China. On the other hand, famed Rinzai masters such as Bankei Yōtaku (1622–93) followed and taught a Zen path without koans. In modern times the celebrated Rinzai master Hakuin Ekaku (1685–1768) gave a new boost to koan practice that persists today. In his school the koans were catalogued according to type and systematized. The koan exercises commonly used now go back to his reforming work.

This systematization of the koan exercises did not bring about a unification of praxis. Since the beginning, there has been a considerable lack of clarity—still unremedied today— concerning the concrete use of the koans by the masters. Doubtless they were not particularly anxious to control the constantly growing wealth of koan materials, being confident of their ability to guide their students as they saw fit. They passed on what they had received, generally useful directions more or less adapted to the individual. The difficulty becomes most apparent when it is a question of judging the progress of a practitioner and finally of recognizing the solution of a koan. The criterion of success is the attainment of the desired state of consciousness, which can be reached by various methods through concrete practice.

We have seen that practice begins with the regulation of sitting and breathing and the effort to concentrate, aided by attention to the breath. As a further aid to attention, a word is given to the practitioner, on which he is to concentrate. In many cases this word is *mu* (literally *not* or *nothing*), the key word of the first koan in the collection *Mumonkan*. Concentration is a precondition of practice, but the koan exercise as such goes beyond mere concentration. Here is the complete text of the first example of the *Mumonkan*, an exchange between master and disciple: "A monk asks Chao-chou: 'Has a dog also got Buddha-nature?' Chao- chou answers: 'Mu'." This exchange clearly contains a cognitive element. The question about the Buddha-nature of the dog can be answered with a yes or a no. So there is a temptation for the practitioner to seek a rational solution. But in vain. A rational solution to a koan cannot suffice, even if some koan examples suggest a plausible cognitive solution.

An intellectual solution cannot bring about the alteration of consciousness aimed at by koan practice, because it remains on the plane of subject-object duality. The practitioner, who has received the koan as an object, occupies himself with this object and seeks the corresponding answer. Some koan questions ("What is the Buddha?", "What is the way?" or "What is the meaning of the coming of the First Patriarch [Bodhidharma] from the West?") touch on what in the Zen view is the ultimate reality. The answers given to the examples are shockingly banal: "Three pounds of flax," "A dried shit-stick," or "The tree in front of the garden." One reason for the illogical character of these replies is the disparity in level between question and answer. The difficulty can be rationally dissolved by assuming, in accordance with Mahāyāna metaphysics, that the highest truth embraces all levels, and by concluding that consequently every answer hits it mark. But that line of thought remains in the rational realm, which has to be broken through in reaching a new stage of consciousness.

It is not easy to attain this breakthrough of the rational sphere. In the Zen literature the psychological process has often been depicted. Finding that his intellectual forces are insufficient, the practitioner feels himself at a loss, as if locked into a narrow space. He runs against the same wall again and again and looks for the way out. But the wall will not yield, and meanwhile the door is open. To see the open door, a turn of one hundred eighty degrees is needed. In an early essay, D. T. Suzuki describes the process according to a schema of accumulation, saturation, and explosion. Other Zen masters have the milder analogy of the chick knocking against the eggshell from within until in the end it breaks. The compiler of *Mumonkan*, Wu-men Hui-k'ai (1183–1260), speaks of the agony of the practitioner who feels as if he has swallowed "a red-hot iron ball, which you cannot spit out even if you try." The gripping passage ends, "When the time comes, the internal and external will be spontaneously united."[26] Note the phrase "when the times comes," which signifies, as Ruth Fuller Sasaki explains, that the koan is resolved when the state of consciousness that the koan aimed to illuminate is reached.[27] This state of consciousness is, as Master Hui-k'ai says, a state of unity. The koan is given to the practitioner as an object of study and practice in order that he will so completely appropriate it that it no longer stands as a separate object. Solution of the koan means to become one with the koan.

Constant gazing at the koan helps the practitioner to become one with it. Here Zen Buddhism brings into play the force of *prajña*, the wisdom that gazes but without beholding an object. The Japanese philosopher and semanticist Izutsu Toshihiko clarified the psychological and semantic aspects of the process:

> Settling into a state of deep, one-pointed concentration, the student must continue gazing at the *Mu*, tenaciously and intensely, repeating at the same time the word *Mu*, silently or loudly, to himself until his whole body and mind, losing itself, gets into a particular state of consciousness at which Jōshu himself is supposed to have uttered the word *Mu!*, beyond the bifurcation of consciousness into subject and object. . . . The peculiar semantic content of the word *mu* (nothing) also contributes a great deal toward inducing in the student a special psychological state in which the subject and the object have coalesced into an absolute unity of pure Awareness.[28]

Christian meditation does not aim at this oneness with the koan but seeks rather a loving union with God, the supreme good (*summum bonum*). Yet the koan method is also of value for Christians because of its human structure. The introduction of this method into the way to enlightenment is a remarkable Chinese contribution, and the underlying moment of questioning and doubt is universally human. The collision with unanswerable questions and the formulation of puzzling, paradoxical, and illogical expressions, including symbolic body language, are everyday events, for humans are questioning beings surrounded by unsolved riddles. It is no surprise that in the Christian tradition, too, there are episodes, sayings, even whole sets of stories that correspond to Zen koans.

The Irish Jesuit William Johnston first, as far as I know, discovered the Christian koan. He saw difficulty, if not danger, for the Christian practitioner in the Zen koan, since it leads deep into the "Buddhist cosmos": "The person who solves the koans one by one

. . . can fairly claim to have imbibed the essentials of Buddhism, to have seen into the essence of things, and be living the life of the Buddha."[29] This insight aroused disquiet among Christian meditation leaders, even though for the most part practitioners fully absorbed in their koan scarcely notice the predominantly Buddhist content of the examples.

Johnston's reflections were intensified by the sense that the Christian tradition, too, must embody this movement from the concentrated anxiety and contradiction of human existence to a spiritually satisfying solution. The natural place to look was the biblical heritage. "I see it [the koan] as a help to the understanding of our Christian Scriptures and as a guide to meditation based upon biblical paradox." He finds Paul, especially, to be "one of the great koan-masters of all time."[30] The Bible indeed offers an abundance of koan material. Moses' puzzlement before the bush that burns without being consumed (Exodus 3), the many paradoxes of the story of David, Jesus' parable of the seed that dies in the earth to bear fruit in a new life, or the story of the camel who can go more easily through the eye of a needle than can a rich man enter the Kingdom of Heaven, are some examples that remain striking even today. Several biblical parables make fun of reason, while the Beatitudes, in their transvaluation of principles, call for a radical turning about.

The greatest Christian koan is the cross. In one of the cases in the *Hekiganroku* the expression "Great Death" denotes the new consciousness that breaks through in Zen enlightenment. According to Gundert, this experience comes to "people, not only in a Buddhist context, for whom all that they are and have breaks down one day, so that they feel as if they are dying. . . . Since it is by their own insight into the nothingness of existence that they are overcome, this is not an incomprehensible, feared, hated, petty dying, but something great."[31] Thomas Merton tells how the word of the cross gives the Christian a radically new consciousness of the meaning of his life and of his relationship to others and the surrounding world.[32] The identification with Christ in the cross and resurrection is the true mystery of the Christian life. In Zen terminology: "By living death with him, one breaks through to resurrection and a Jesus-enlighten-ment."[33]

The Christian koan finds its climax in becoming one with Christ, the Lord. The Japanese Jesuit Kadowaki Kakichi teaches a koan, *shu* (literally, *Lord*), inspired by the early Christian Kyrios.[34] Instead of mu, which allows him to become one with nothing, the practitioner recites in rhythm with his breathing the similar-sounding word *shu*. "At the beginning the breathing takes the lead but gradually the *shu* becomes the subject of the rhythmical breathing. . . . Breath and *shu* become one." The practitioner feels himself to be embraced by the Lord and lives in the Lord, fulfilling the Pauline word: "I live, no longer I, but Christ lives in me" (Gal. 2.20). This Christianizing of the koan has not gone uncontested, but it demonstrates a real possibility.

Because of its different schools, lineages, and Zen masters them-selves, whose individuality carries great weight, Zen Buddhism has since early on encompassed a plurality of ways to deal with the koan. Koan practice is impossible, even dangerous, if, in one's solitary practice (Japanese: *dokusan*), one lacks the guidance of the master (Japanese: *rōshi*). In the course of the centuries there have been many ups and downs, extreme cases, and phenomena of decline. Merton's warning that koan study tends to formalization and institutionaliza-tion is especially pertinent today.[35] When hundreds of koans are worked through at the greatest speed, one can hardly expect a lasting effect. Practice is reduced to the completion of a course requirement or a program and no attention is paid to Hakuin's teaching on the relation between doubt and experience: Where doubt is strong, enlightenment is also great. The koan method can be varied in many ways but must not degenerate to a soulless technique or frivolous game-playing. As we noted at the start, it is not necessarily required for Zen meditation. As in Buddhism, there are also Christian Zen masters who content themselves with the basic practice and meditation "without thought or images." The koan method is psychologically, historically, and spiritually significant, and it remains an important task to investigate it in depth.

INTERPRETING ZEN ENLIGHTENMENT

In all higher religions, spiritual experiences occur that go far beyond the everyday and are designated by scholars of religion as "mystical" in a broad sense. Japanese use this word only reluctantly for the enlightenment experience of Zen Buddhism, since in their language the word "mystical" suggests the esoteric. D. T. Suzuki repeatedly expresses his aversion to the word, but in the meantime there has been a marked change in usage in Japan. Today we can confidently categorize Zen enlightenment as one of the phenomena designated as mystical in the science of religions.

The Japanese word for enlightenment, *satori*, denotes a supersensible knowing that goes beyond ordinary thinking. Zen circles prefer the word *kenshō*, which means the vision of the essence, or of the self, or of one's own nature. In addition, the Sino-Japanese compound *daigo* is often found in the Zen literature; it literally means the "great illumination" experienced by a Zen master when his struggle with a difficult koan issues in a breakthrough.

The history of religion tells of many different kinds of mystical experience. In many religions the metaphor of light is used, whereby the experience is characterized as one of illumination. Mystical experience, as the Greek root *muein* (from which *mysterion* comes) shows, is mysterious, literally ungraspable and unsayable. It is as clear in Buddhism as in Christianity that mystery is of the essence of religion. The basic Buddhist image of enlightenment is the experience of the founder Shākyamuni, who awoke to Buddhahood under the pippala tree. He is the perfectly enlightened one. Every Buddhist, including the meditating Zen Buddhist, looks up to him and strives to emulate him. The Zen experience is intimately related to the many forms of enlightenment that have been attained during the more than two thousand years of Buddhist history.

The Zen experience of enlightenment, after centuries of transmission, is still a living presence. Though we cannot say with certainty that the cases of enlightenment related in early Zen chronicles coincide with experiences in today's Zen monasteries and Zen halls, there is an astonishing resemblance. The experience in all cases is unutterable. Descriptions in early reports, which focus on the words of the Zen masters, and detailed explanations in more recent works converge to delineate the stages leading to the experience and its aftermath. The tone differs greatly from case to case. Some experiences open up quietly, as a bud blossoms in obscurity; others terrify with their suddenness. In the reports of practitioners, stereotyped expressions recur, perhaps stemming from the master. There is an overwhelmingly strong feeling that all is one. The "little I" has disappeared and the "great I" spreads out infinitely. Since most practitioners have engaged intensively with the koan of nothingness, it is not surprising that, for them, all becomes nothing or nothing becomes all. Often the successful breakthrough is accompanied by a sheer and ecstatic joy.

The explanatory remarks of recognized masters lead deeper into the heart of enlightenment. D. T. Suzuki emphasizes the turnaround through which a new point of view is reached. "Satori is the sudden flashing into new consciousness of a new truth hitherto undreamed of. . . . Religiously, it is a new birth; intellectually, it is the acquiring of a new viewpoint. The world now appears as if dressed in a new garment, which seems to cover up all the unsightliness of dualism, which is called delusion in Buddhist phraseology."[36] In the new viewpoint all things appear as transformed: "Satori is a sort of inner perception—not the perception, indeed, of a single individual object. The ultimate destination of satori is towards the Self."[37]

Shibayama Zenkei (1894–1974), the abbot of Nanzenji Temple in Kyoto who died a few years ago, was one of the great Japanese Zen masters of this century. He analyzed and evaluated the remarks of Wu-men Hui-k'ai on the first koan of the *Mumonkan* in a commentary that is typical of Japanese Zen. This long text, which in contrast to the terse remarks on the other koans is a weighty document, stands out remarkably in the peaceful course of the work. The Chinese master praises the "wonderful enlightenment" to which the practitioner comes through "the gateless barrier." "To attain the wonderful enlightenment, one must completely cut off the stirrings of consciousness." Shibayama explains this unconditional demand: " . . . one has to cut his ordinary self away and be reborn as a new Self in a different dimension. In other words, the student must personally have the inner experience called satori, by which he is reborn as the True Self. This fundamental experience of awakening is essential in Zen. Although various different expressions are used when talking about the fact of this religious awakening, it cannot be real Zen without it." The equation of enlightenment with the experience of the True Self corresponds to the tradition of the Sixth Patriarch, normative in Japanese Zen Buddhism; he uses the expression *kenshō*, that is, a "vision of the essence or (one's own) nature." The True Self, also called the original face one had before birth, is identical with the essence or nature. The vision is not possible without breaking through the barrier of the stirrings of consciousness called forth by discriminative thinking. Wu-men incessantly calls for the cutting off of all dualistic stirrings. Though this is painful, it makes the resulting enlightenment all the more attractive. "Mumon tells us how wonderful it is to experience breaking through the barrier and to live the life of satori. Once the Gate is broken through, ultimate peace is attained. You can get hold of old Jōshū alive. Further, you will live in the same spirituality with all the Zen Masters, see them face to face, and enjoy the Truth of Oneness. How wonderful, how splendid!"

And Wu-men teaches how this satori is attained. Extreme effort is required, so that in becoming one with the koan both *mu* and self are transcended. "Needless to say it has nothing to do with intellectual discrimination or dualistic reasoning. It is utterly beyond all description." In Wu-men's text the ineffability of the experience is expressed through the metaphor of the dream of a deaf person, which no one else can know. Correspondingly, the experience can be attained only by the most personal deed of the practitioner. The breakthrough happens suddenly—the text also notes this essential trait of satori—and grants an unknown, sovereign freedom. The Master of Nanzenji, encouraging his disciples, calls to mind the essential traits of satori: "For the one who has passed through the abyss of Great Doubt, transcending subject and object, you and I, and has been revived as the True Self, can there be anything to disturb him?. . . How wonderful it is to live such a serene life with perfect freedom, the spiritual freedom of the one who has attained religious peace."[38] Master Wu-men concludes with a metaphor of light: the experience is like the kindling of a "Dharma-light," which symbolizes "the light of the self," according to Asahina Sōgen, abbot of Engakuji temple.[39]

In an afterword to the first volume of his disciples' reports of their experiences, Zen master Yasutani Hakuun of the Harada line explains in concentrated terms the experience of enlightenment:

> Enlightenment signifies seeing through one's own essen-
> tial nature, and this means at the same time seeing through
> the essential nature of the cosmos and of all things. For
> seeing through the essential nature is the wisdom of en-
> lightenment. One may call the essential nature truth if one
> wishes. In Buddhism from early on it has been called
> thusness or the Buddha-nature or the One Mind. In Zen
> it is also called Nothing, the one hand or the original face,
> differing epithets for an identical content.[40]

Yasutani stresses the cosmic dimension of Zen enlightenment and relates it to the worldview of Buddhist East Asia as shaped by the Mahāyāna sutras. His listing of the three fundamental koans of Zen Buddhism in the last sentence shows the close link between satori and koan practices. Enlightenment and the koan reflect the same vision of the world.

In their accounts of enlightenment, the Zen masters refer to reports transmitted in the literature and to what they themselves have undergone, repeatedly stressing that any account falls far short of the ineffable experience. Drawing on a living acquaintance with the tradition, they can complete and illuminate their explanations with anecdotes and descriptions from their monastic lives, against the spiritual background furnished by the Mahāyāna sutras and the concretization of their wisdom in the koans.

Paramount for Zen praxis is the warning, often repeated to pupils, not to seek extraordinary experiences, combined with encouragement of the most intense effort. This paradoxical combination is rooted in Buddhist tradition. Since its earliest days, Buddhism has urged prudence in dealing with supersensible mental gifts. In Zen the serene and patient attitude toward unusual experiences is based on the conviction that enlightenment is not the fruit of one's own endeavor but the apprehension of the True Self or one's original nature—in religious terms the Buddha-nature—that reveals itself when the moment has come, the moment of maturation that withdraws itself from the power of the practitioner. Impatient expectation is a hindrance. The attitude known as *taigo-Zen* (Zen that expects enlightenment) is generally rejected in Zen. Objectless meditation, linked with the purifying and emptying of consciousness, is the appropriate preparation for deeper experiences.

One should also note the distinctions of degrees and stages of enlightenment. The lowest degrees are not recognized by all masters as belonging to enlightenment, since they often involve only momentary stirrings that disappear quickly on returning to the everyday. Great enlightenments are at all times rare. There are impressive accounts of such happenings in the Zen literature. Their significance should be measured by their effects.

These practical remarks are crucial in the assessment of Christian Zen practice. Still less than Zen Buddhists should Christians strive after extraordinary states of consciousness. If depth-experiences emerge in the course of zealous practice, they should be thankfully accepted and taken as spurs to greater effort. More profoundly, the attitude of patient waiting corresponds entirely to Christian spirituality. The French Jesuit Yves Raguin sees Zen meditation and Zen enlightenment in this Christian perspective. He writes:

> Being a child of the Father, I learned from Christ to be simply attentive to my inner mystery, knowing that I cannot see my face as God's child, unless the Father en-

lightens me by his own Spirit. The practice of Zen meditation taught me to stay in pure attentiveness before my
inner mystery. . . . In fact it is the practice of Zen which
helped me to understand that the final step is not to follow
Christ or to imitate him, but to be animated by him,
because he lives in us.[41]

The leaders of Christian Zen meditation explicitly warn disciples
against the quest for unusual experiences, especially widespread
today though it has always existed everywhere. The Zen tradition
tells of spiritual men who tore up or threw away the certificate of
attainment of enlightenment before the very eyes of their master. In
all religions the historical picture is disfigured by human arrogance
or formality despite confirmed and practiced casting off of the ego.
Christians should see their Zen practice as a way to union with God.

The profound experiences a person enjoys on the way to spiritual
maturity correspond to the religion in which he is inwardly most
strongly rooted. For the Christian, this is not the experience of Zen
enlightenment; according to reliable Zen masters, whom we must
suppose to be enlightened, Zen enlightenment is an impersonal
experience of the True Self, considered to be identical with original
nature or the Buddha-nature and so with the cosmos, an experience
which excludes duality. Zen enlightenment, seen by adherents of the
school as the quintessence of their religion, is thus irreconcilable with
the Christian belief in a personal creator God and in the redemptive
act of Christ, rooted in divine mercy. Enomiya-Lassalle locates the
difference between Zen and Christian experience chiefly in the
apersonal character of the Zen experience. He is convinced that in
both cases "absolute and undivided being is experienced. . . . The
distinction resides in the fact that the Zen experience is an apersonal

one, while the Christian experience is a personal apprehension of the absolute. The responsive feeling of the recipient is so different that there must also be some essential distinction in the phenomenon itself."[42] This is confirmed by the insistence of Zen Buddhists on the experience of satori as an undiluted unity that excludes all differentiation. The unity of reality, they say, leaves no trace of duality behind. Against this, Enomiya-Lassalle, who has the deepest understanding of the human longing for unity, persuasively claims in religious terms that there must be something further:

> the authentic absolute, transcendent in the fullest sense. However close the relation between God and creature may be—so close that it can be expressed clearly in words only at the risk of making it an identity; one need only think of the paradoxes of Eckhart!—there nonetheless remains a distance, and one which is infinite: if God did not exist there would be no creatures, but the converse does not hold: In the case that not a single atom of the entire universe existed, God would not on that account be less by a single hair than he now is with the whole universe. Hence the Christian, as long as he retains his belief in God, will not be persuaded to relinquish this view even by an experience of satori. To the contrary, he will live this experience as a being-one with God and thus will rather be strengthened in his faith in God.[43]

One may justifiably ask whether this Christian experience of being one with God can be called a satori experience. The distinction between the Christian and the Zen experience is comprehensive and fundamental. It can scarcely be grasped in terms of a description of the phenomena, as these are ineffable; yet it emerges all the more clearly at the level of interpretation. As the expert on ascesis and mysticism Josef Sudbrack has often pointed out, the contrast between personal and apersonal points up the difference between the entire worldview of Mahāyāna Buddhism and the Christian faith in revelation. Here further theological investigations, which lie beyond the framework of this chapter, are required.

Zen meditation is rich in values that appeal to Christians. Thus, Christians and Zen Buddhists quickly developed friendly relations, undisturbed even by the occasional collision. People who are serious about their religion are never attracted by syncretism; they want to move from mere tolerance to genuine contact with the adherents of other religions. Zen Buddhists and Christians have been enriched in various ways by their contact and have learned much of importance from one another, and further solid bridges of mutual understanding are certainly desirable.

BRIDGES OF UNDERSTANDING

At the Second Vatican Council (1962–65), the Catholic Church opened itself to the world and encouraged a new attitude toward the world religions. The Christian-Buddhist dialogue that was launched then has been strongly affected by the Zen Buddhist emphasis on meditation. Adherents of both faiths are traveling a part of the way together. The basic practice of meditation can be accomplished in unison, allowing the sort of contact that promotes mutual understanding. Zen Buddhists and Christians come to know one another as serious religious people who cherish and cultivate spiritual values despite the consumerist materialism of our times, people who seek salvation and are ready for rigorous and constant practice.

As it proceeds further, meditation leads practitioners onto different paths, yet the objectless meditation transmitted in Zen is also possible for Christians. As Raguin writes: "No thinking could make me realize this inner mystery of mind. I could not rely on any thought, any desire, to reach this presence of God in me."[44] The inner purification of consciousness from thoughts and images, far from causing a desolate void, can create a space for profound experiences that are normally expressed in negative terms in Zen.

Here a way to deeper understanding opens up. The "nothing" on which Zen Buddhists focus in their meditation is neither a nihilistic nothingness nor an ontological non-being in opposition to being, but rather a reality that surpasses the categories of being and non-being. Practice yields no philosophical reflections, yet in the atmosphere of the Zen hall, Christians can feel something of "the fullness of nothingness." It is entirely desirable that Christians acquire a knowledge of the intellectual foundations of Buddhism, particularly the doctrines of the *Perfection of Wisdom Sutras*. They will notice that in the West, too, there is a negative way, going back to Philo (25 B.C.E.–50 C.E.) and Plotinus (204–69) and to the Greek fathers of the Church, who reinterpreted Neo-Platonic ideas to formulate a negative theology centered on the incomprehensibility of God's infinite essence. Christian mystics, full of the incomprehensible mystery of God, frequently have recourse to negative terms to express it.

In shared practice, the Christian cannot help noticing the uncommonly refined feeling for nature of the Japanese Zen Buddhists, who feel themselves in accord with their natural surroundings as they practice. We have seen that the Zen enlightenment has a cosmic element: the human being knows himself as microcosmos in unity with the macrocosmos. Here the Christian encounters a dimension with which he is less familiar but which can become a bridge to understanding. The cosmic sense of nature has strongly revived in the West in our days. In his later years, Romano Guardini struggled for a personal understanding of the cosmos.[45] The real discoverer of the significance of the cosmic for Christian thought and feeling in our time is Teilhard de Chardin (1881–1955), who enjoyed a vivid cosmic awareness not only as a scientist but as a theologian and religious thinker and clearly showed in his work that this awareness could be united with Christian theism.[46] An attentive, meditative reading of the Pauline Epistles can greatly help the Christian to acquire a cosmic sense. Pauline theology witnesses to Christ, the risen Lord, as the personal head of the cosmos, a truth found in Christian tradition in every century. If contact with Zen Buddhists awakens Christians to a living relation with the cosmic Christ, this certainly enriches their religious lives.

For all its high flights, Zen meditation never loses contact with the everyday, the earth under its feet. "Ordinary mind is the way," according to a koan in the *Mumonkan*.[47] The way—the Tao, the cosmic principle of the universe—also guides human beings' behavior in all situations. It is not only in the Zen hall that Zen disciples use zazen; their "mind in action" meditates constantly, and the meditation is entirely bound up with everyday life. Zen master Yasutani Hakuun sums up the meaning of this koan in the question, "Is not everything that a person does from morning to evening, just as it is, the way?" The everyday mind, his commentary tells us, is "the restful, constant, peaceful mind, undisturbed by external things." The koan urges continued practice in everyday life after one has achieved the first sudden enlightenment. As Wu-men insists, the experienced person should "still practice for thirty years, then he will understand completely." This means that practice, correctly understood, has no end. The human being is a practitioner his life long. It is unnecessary to point out how closely this corresponds with the

Christian concept of ascesis. The *homo viator* must tirelessly stride forward on the spiritual way. This realization that one is, in a deep sense, a wayfarer is a precious fruit of shared practice.

The bridges of understanding have been tested in everyday life by Zen and Christian monks in their extended reciprocal visits in Europe (1979) and Japan (1983).[48] In the first visit the Japanese monks, divided into small groups of three to six, spent about three weeks in Benedictine and Cistercian monasteries in Germany, Holland, Belgium, France, and Italy, sharing the monks' daily schedule from morning to evening, including prayer in the chapel, meals in the refectory, physical work in garden or field, and recreation in fraternal dialogue. As reports and occasional answers to inquiries indicate, the Japanese visitors were very impressed by the fact that the highly cultivated Christian monks spent a few hours daily on physical work, just like Buddhists. The "pray and work" (*ora et labora*) of the Benedictine rule, a foundation of Western Christian culture, corresponds to the Zen monastic rule developed in T'ang China (618–907) which also made a place in the daily schedule for physical service (Japanese: *samu*) in the form of work in the field, garden, or house. In both traditions physical work is an essential part of the spiritual way. The Japanese Zen Buddhists did not need to be told about the meaning and value of this work. One Japanese monk relates that the busy monks had little time for discussion, but "to welcome us as members of their community to the deepest recesses of their lives without hiding or embellishing a thing, and to show us the back as well as the front of things, that in itself was ten times more meaningful than to try to make us understand things through formal dialogues. These monks have understood that in their spiritual wisdom." Another monk felt that his religious life was enriched by what he calls—with a touch of poetic refinement—the "mutual echo" (*hibiki-ai*) in the encounter of the two authentic spiritual traditions of East and West.

The return visit of the Christian nuns and monks was different in several respects. The group was smaller, fifteen men and two women, and, as the program required, all had some experience with Zen meditation. Nevertheless, they found the initial seven days of practice in a temple in central Japan extremely painful. The unremitting severity of the *sesshin*, which went far beyond what they had experienced in Zen courses in Europe, pushed the visitors, some of whom were elderly, to the edge of physical endurance. After this first difficult week, they visited some famous monasteries, and the Japanese showered consideration upon their Western guests. The European monks spent the last week in small groups in a Zen monastery, while the sisters stayed at a female monastery of the Sōtō school.

From the reports of the Christian nuns and monks on their experiences in the Zen monastery, let us examine just two impressions. Not a few of the Western visitors were irritated by what one of them refers to as the "antiquated formalism" of the "ritualistic lifestyle" with its multitude of minutely detailed rules and usages: "The rules seemed to be inflexible; the law mattered more than the person." Some recalled their own novitiate. In answer to their query, Zen masters replied that such rigor was necessary to train their students and help them conquer self-centeredness.

Another observation made by the Christian monks dealt with a deeper realm. They noted with astonishment the large role of cult and worship in Zen monastic life: "We were impressed," writes one, "by the serious participation of the Zen monks in the sutra chantings and ceremonies. . . . We were struck by the religious character of the Zen hall." And another: "Respect for the sacred plays an important role in the Japanese monasteries." The Christian monks evidently found it difficult to reconcile this essential trait of Zen spirituality with their previous conceptions. We have already made some suggestions as to the solution of this dilemma and can content ourselves here with noting this cultic respect and its accompanying appreciation of religious symbolism as another bridge to understanding.

The reciprocal visits of Zen and Christian monks continue. Pope John Paul II expressed his delight at this initiative. When the first Buddhists visited Rome, he said, "I rejoice that the interreligious dialogue is moving on this basic spiritual level. This kind of experience must continue."[49]

The encounter with Zen stands out in the dialogue between Christianity and the world religions because it is not confined to theoretical discussion but involves religious praxis. Christians and Zen Buddhists have learned from one another in practical activities. The deepening of this mutual influence, through further intelligent endeavors, remains desirable.

Recent years have seen a variety of divergent views about the Christian-Buddhist dialogue. These have been accompanied, in some quarters, by a surfacing of theological qualms. The relationship between the two traditions is mutually challenging; the coexistence of Zen and Christianity gives rise to a pluralism that many find confusing and even disturbing, but it is bound to generate new paths of spiritual exploration. At the moment, we are in an experimental phase. A revival of the great tradition of Christian mysticism seems an essential prerequisite for future progress. Awareness of this tradition will give Christians the confidence, courage, and critical discernible—what St. Ignatius calls "discernment of spirits"—that are needed as the dialogue continues into the twenty-first century.

EPILOGUE

A fter the second volume of my history of Zen Buddhism appeared, friends and sympathizers of the Zen movement often asked me why I had concluded my work with the beginning of the twentieth century, despite the fact that the new and fascinating questions then opened up call so pressingly for emphatic investigation and decisive clarification. However, I had replied to these well-meaning demands in advance in the epilogue to my second volume, where I noted that the constantly expanding pluralism brought about by Zen's entry into the West eluded historical summary, at least for the present. Accordingly, the modest volume presented here is not a historical study, though the various questions it poses and the manner in which it develops them are determined by the eminently historical event of the Western reception of Zen, from which our discussion began. I have not aimed at a continuation of the history of Zen but wish merely to point out some of the striking aspects of the Zen movement in the twentieth century, all of which are connected in some way with the spectacular echo Zen has found in the West. Nor is the survey in any way comprehensive. The selection of topics was limited, and the views expressed vary according to my experience of and relation to the respective topics.

When we consider the influences received and the effects produced by Zen in the West, two circumstances are particularly striking. First, the Zen movement strikes at the very heart of contemporary life and addresses the most pressing needs of our times. Hence the speed with which it has taken root and drawn numerous followers. A pervasive sense that "the times are out of joint" has led many people to turn away from the stress of external impressions and to seek their identity, their self, so as to find peace and security. Asia's words of wisdom about "rest in movement" and "movement in rest" have opened many doors to the Zen way that incarnates this wisdom. The stillness attained in earnest, silent meditation helps us find the solution to the great anxieties of our time. To Westerners who have lost their equilibrium, Zen teaches an attitude that integrally embraces body and mind and is experienced psychologically as a new consciousness. This too is strikingly in accord with contemporary currents, including some of those that have found their way into the mixed bag of New Age sensibilities. Japanese Zen masters have kept a marked distance from the New Age movement, not because they fail to recognize the reality and urgency of the issues addressed, but because they wish to preserve the character proper to the Zen way. The essential questions have been clearly articulated in the Zen schools. Following the Japanese Zen masters, we have seen that Zen in this century illuminates the central problems of Eastern and Western cultures. Zen will continue to play a guiding role in the encounter of the two hemispheres and in the intensive study and personal engagement this encounter demands of us.

Second, we are struck by the plurality of forms of religious praxis that Zen has generated and that contemporary research has brought fully into view. An unexpected abundance of information on the early history of Chinese Ch'an and the originality and diversity of the great figures of the T'ang period has come to light. This pluralism of Ch'an takes a stronger form in the opposing tendencies of the Zen houses and schools that developed later. In Japan, pluralism is marked by a tendency to syncretistic combinations, for example, when Zen temples integrate such forms of religious praxis as the esoteric rites of Shingon or the invocation of the name of Amida. Throughout the centuries one can follow the battle against this admixture of alien elements. Dōgen, for example, insisted on the purity of Zen as he had appropriated it in China; yet even in his own Sōtō school Shingon practices were widely accepted. Meanwhile, many shrewd Japanese Zen masters recognized the usefulness of the *nembutsu* and refrained from troubling their faithful who practiced this devotion.

The reception of Zen meditation in the West has led to a broad spectrum of theological hypotheses and practical forms of spiritual exercise. New formations of every kind have been invented in Western Zen centers, and groups with radically different worldviews have interpreted the newly discovered ways according to their outlooks, with corresponding practices. Christian meditation leaders, too, have brought their own views and preferences into play in their practice, uniting Christian motifs with Zen meditation in various ways. We are in the initial stages of this plurality. The great desideratum is that East and West come together in spiritual harmony. This is a difficult challenge, for humanity is exposed as never before to distractions of every sort. The rampant multiplication of forms of Zen praxis poses the question as to what degree of pluralism is compatible with a genuine continuation of the tradition. Zen Buddhists, conscious of their roots, claim the name "Zen" for their schools, yet many of them also want to insist on the universality of what that name denotes. On the spiritual path human beings need a free space that permits them to find their way toward the goal of a fulfilled life and to unity with ultimate reality and the highest good. But pluralism must not be the pretext for a dissipation of spiritual energies in arbitrariness. In fidelity to the truth of their nature, following the guidance of the light that is granted them, and impelled by the restlessness of their hearts, may all wayfaring humans find that peace and fulfillment that resides in eternal truth.

NOTES

CHAPTER ONE

1. Masao Abe, ed., *A Zen Life: D. T. Suzuki Remembered* (New York, Tokyo: Weatherhill, 1986), p. 21. This work contains a useful chronology and a bibliography (pp. 219–24, 235–46). See also the biographical data in H. Rzepowski, *Das Menschenbild bei Daisetsu Teitaro Suzuki* (St. Augustin, 1971).

2. Rudolf Otto, *Das Gefühl des Überweltlichen* (Munich: Beck, 1931), pp. 242–43.

CHAPTER TWO

1. "Shamon Dōgen," in *Watsuji Tetsurō Zenshū* (*Collected Works of Watsuji Tetsurō*) (Tokyo, 1977), IV, pp. 156–246; quotation, pp. 156ff.

2. Ibid., p. 160.

3. "*Shōbōgenzō* no Tetsugaku Shikan," in Tanabe's *Zenshū* (Tokyo, 1963), V, pp. 443–94: quotations, pp. 445, 451. The essay first appeared in 1939.

4. *Dōgen no Kenkyū* (Tokyo, 1935).

5. Hee-Jin Kim, *Dōgen Kigen: Mystical Realist* (Tucson: University of Arizona Press, 1975).

6. Etō Sukuo, *Shūso Toshite no Dōgen Zenji* (Tokyo, 1944).

149

7. Masunaga Reihō, *The Sōtō Approach to Zen* (Tokyo, 1948), p. 193. We owe to Masunaga the English translation of an important writing from Dōgen's school: *A Primer of Sōtō Zen: A Translation of Dōgen's Shōbōgenzō Zuimonki* (Honolulu: East-West Center, 1971).

8. Heinrich Dumoulin, "Die religiöse Metaphysik des Japanischen Zen-Meisters Dōgen," *Saeculum* 12 (1961), pp. 205–36.

9. *Eastern Buddhist* 4:1 (1971), pp. 28–71.

10. Kim, *Dōgen Kigen*, p. 98.

11. "The Incomparable Philosopher: Dōgen on How to Read the *Shōbōgenzō*," in *Dōgen Studies*, ed. William R. LaFleur (Honolulu, 1985), pp. 83–98; quotations, pp. 89, 83, 85, 91.

12. See the quotation from "Mitsugo" in Kim, *Dōgen Kigen*, p. 108.

13. For a survey of the Kyoto school see Fritz Buri, *Der Buddha-Christus als der Herr des wahren Selbst: Die Religionsphilosophie der Kyoto-Schule und das Christentum* (Bern and Stuttgart, 1982). The Nanzan Institute for Religion and Culture of Nanzan University in Nagoya has made available much valuable material on the Kyoto school in its publications and symposia.

14. For an introduction to his life and work see Buri, *Buddha-Christus*, pp. 53–80; G. K. Piovesana, *Recent Japanese Philosophical Thought 1862–1962*, revised edition (Tokyo, 1968), pp. 85–122. Nishida's complete works in seventeen volumes appeared in Tokyo in 1965–66.

15. Nishida Kitarō, *An Inquiry into the Good*, trans. Masao Abe and Christopher Ives (Yale University Press, 1990).

16. Quoted in Buri, *Buddha-Christus*, p. 58. See Takeuchi Yoshinori, "The Philosophy of Nishida," in *The Buddha Eye: An Anthology of the Kyoto School*, ed. Frederick Franck (New York, 1982), pp. 179–202. Takeuchi writes that "in him Japan has had the first philosophical genius who knew how to build a system permeated with the spirit of

Buddhist meditation, by fully employing the Western way of thinking" (p. 181).

17. Nishida Kitarō, *Intuition and Reflection in Self-Consciousness*, trans. Y. Takeuchi, V. Vigielmo, J. S. O'Leary (State University of New York Press, 1987).

18. Nishida Kitarō, *Art and Morality*, trans. David Dilworth and Valdo Viglielmo (Honolulu: East-West Center, 1973).

(There is no English translation of *From the Acting to the Seeing*.)

19. Nishida Kitarō, *Fundamental Problems of Philosophy*, trans. D. Dilworth (Tokyo: Sophia University, 1970).

20. "The Self-Identity of Absolute Contradictories" is translated as "The Unity of Opposites" by Robert Schinzinger, in Nishida, *Intelligibility and the Philosophy of Nothingness* (Tokyo: Maruzen, 1958). This volume also includes "The Intelligible World" and "Goethe's Metaphysical Background." Also in German translation is "Was liegt dem Selbstsein zugrunde?," trans. S. Yagi in *Gott in Japan*, ed. S. Yagi and U. Luz (Munich, 1973), pp. 94–112.

21. Nishida Kitarō, "Towards a Philosophy of Religion with the Concept of Pre-Established Harmony as Guide," trans. D. Dilworth, in *Eastern Buddhist* 3:1 (1970), pp. 19–46.

22. Nishida Kitarō, "The Logic of the Place of Nothingness and the Religious Worldview," trans. D. Dilworth in *Last Writings: Nothingness and the Religious Worldview* (Honolulu: University of Hawaii Press, 1987).

23. Nishida, "Towards a Philosophy of Religion," pp. 23, 41, 40.

24. Ibid., pp. 44–45.

25. Nishida, quoted in Dilworth, trans., *Last Writings*, p. 90.

26. Ibid., p. 85.

27. Ibid., p. 88.

28. Ibid., p. 48.

29. Ibid., pp. 69–70.

30. Ibid., pp. 79, 100–101.

31. On Tanabe see Buri, *Buddha-Christus*, pp. 81–112; Piovesana, *Recent Japanese Philosophical Thought*, pp. 145–58, and the excellent introduction by James W. Heisig to his translation of Tanabe's chief work, *Philosophy as Metanoetics* (Berkeley and Los Angeles: University of California Press, 1986). This work has been discussed in a collection of essays, *The Religious Philosophy of Tanabe Hajime: The Metanoetic Imperative*, ed. Taitetsu Unno and James W. Heisig (Berkeley: Asian Humanities Press, 1990). See also Johannes Laube, *Dialektik der absoluten Vermittlung: Hajime Tanabes Religionsphilosophie als Beitrag zum 'Wettstreit der Liebe' zwischen Buddhismus und Christentum* (Freiburg, 1984), with the extensive review of James W. Heisig in *Monumenta Nipponica* 40 (1985), pp. 115–18. Tanabe's collected works in fifteen volumes appeared in Tokyo 1963–64 (reprinted 1972–73).

32. Tanabe Hajime, "The Logic of Species as Dialectics," trans. David Dilworth and Taira Sato, *Monumenta Nipponica* 24 (1969), pp. 273–88.

33. Tanabe, *Philosophy as Metanoetics*, pp. l–li.

34. Ibid., pp. liii, liv.

35. Ibid., p. xxi.

36. Ibid., p. xli.

37. Ibid., p. 170.

38. Ibid., pp. 188, 172; see also pp. 131, 171.

39. German translation in *Martin Heidegger zum 70. Geburtstag* (Pfullingen: Neske, 1959), pp. 93–133.

40. "Memento Mori," trans. Seiichi Yagi (in German) in S. Yagi and Ulrich Luz, eds., *Gott in Japan* (Munich, 1973), pp. 113–26; here pp. 116–17.

41. Ibid., p. 122.

42. Heisig, *Philosophy as Metanoetics*, p. vii.

43.   Heisig's stimulating and convincing portrait of Tanabe's personality provides interesting details on this tense relationship. See *Philosophy as Metanoetics*, p. xiii.

44.   Shimomura Torataro, "D. T. Suzuki's Place in the History of Human Thought," in Abe, ed., *A Zen Life*, pp. 65–80; quotations, pp. 75, 79, 77. See also Buri's discussion of Suzuki in *Buddha-Christus*, pp. 113–42.

45.   *Outlines of Mahāyāna Buddhism* (London, 1907); *Studies in the Lankāvatāra Sutra* (London, 1930); *The Lankāvatāra Sutra: A Translation from the Original Sanskrit* (London, 1932); *The Essence of Buddhism* (London, 1947).

46.   *Rinzai no Kihon Shisō* (Tokyo, 1953). Akizuki Ryōmin gives a special place to this study in his book *Suzuki Zengaku to Nishida Tetsugaku* (*Suzuki's Zen Studies and Nishida's Philosophy*) (Tokyo, 1971).

47.   D. T. Suzuki, *The Zen Doctrine of No-Mind* (London, 1949).

48.   Erich Fromm, D. T. Suzuki, and Richard DeMartino, *Zen Buddhism and Psychoanalysis* (New York: Harper and Row, 1960).

49.   See Buri, *Buddha-Christus*, pp. 143–89; the biographical data in Shin'ichi Hisamatsu, *Die Fülle des Nichts: Vom Wesen des Zen* (Pfullingen: Neske, 1975), pp. 66–67, and *Die Fünf Stände* (Pfullingen: Neske, 1980), pp. 87ff; and the prefatory note to his article "Zen and the Negation of Holiness" in Franck, *Buddha Eye*, pp. 169–70.

50.   Hisamatsu, *Die Fülle des Nichts*, pp. 22, 9, 13.

51.   Buri, *Buddha-Christus*, pp. 145, 149.

52.   See Hisamatsu, "Satori (Selbsterwachen)" in Yagi and Luz, *Gott in Japan*, pp. 127–38; here pp. 134–35.

53.   See Hisamatsu, "Atheismus," *Zeitschrift für Missions- und Religionsgeschichte* 62 (1978), pp. 268–96; here pp. 275ff. See also the instructive prefatory notes of Hans Waldenfels, pp. 268–72.

54. *Die Fülle des Nichts*, pp. 25, 21–23, 39.

55. Yagi and Luz, *Gott in Japan*, p. 135, 137.

56. *Zeitschrift für Missions- und Religionsgeschichte* 62 (1978), pp. 273–74, 279–82, 288–89, 294, 291, 287.

57. *The Heart of Buddhism: In Search of the Timeless Spirit of Primitive Buddhism* (New York: Crossroad, 1983); on Takeuchi, see Buri, *Buddha-Christus*, pp. 255–83.

58. See Buri, *Buddha-Christus*, pp. 191–253; Piovesana, *Recent Japanese Philosophical Thought*, pp. 192–93, 200–204. Hans Waldenfels, *Absolute Nothingness: Foundations of a Buddhist-Christian Dialogue*, trans. J. W. Heisig (New York: Paulist Press, 1980), is an excellent introduction to Nishitani's philosophy of religion; Nishitani in his preface praises Waldenfels as the first Westerner to grasp in depth the core issues in the dialogue between Christianity and Buddhism.

59. The standard English translation, prepared over many years under Nishitani's guidance, is the work of the director of the Nanzan Institute for Religion and Culture, Jan Van Bragt: *Religion and Nothingness* (Berkeley and Los Angeles: University of California Press, 1982). The excellent German translation by Dora Fischer-Barnicol, with a laudatory preface by Nishitani, appeared in the same year: *Was ist Religion?* (Frankfurt, 1982). For discussion of this work see *The Religious Philosophy of Nishitani Keiji: Encounter with Emptiness*, ed. Taitetsu Unno (Berkeley: Asian Humanities Press, 1989).

60. Now available in English translation in: Nishitani Keiji, *Nishida Kitarō*, trans. Yamamoto Seikaku and James W. Heisig (University of California Press, 1991).

61. For these details about Nishitani's schooldays, I have relied on the instructive account in Japanese in Sasaki Toru, *Nishitani Keiji: A Guide to his Thought* (Tokyo, 1986); quotes, pp. 17–23, 32–33, 73.

62. Nishitani, "Watakushi no Tetsugakuteki Hossokuten," in the collection *Kōza Tetsugaku Taikei*, vol. I (Tokyo, 1963), pp. 221–30;

quotes, pp. 221, 229, 226, 227. The text includes several Zen expressions such as *daigi* (Great Doubt) and *ari no mama* (things just as they are); the word *Zen* occurs only once, p. 225.

63. Jan Van Bragt, "Nishitani on Japanese Religiosity," in Joseph Spae, *Japanese Religiosity* (Tokyo, 1971), pp. 271–84 (here p. 279).

64. Nishitani, "The Standpoint of Zen," *Eastern Buddhist* 17:1 (1984), pp. 1–26; quotes, pp. 1, 14, 10.

65. In Franck, *Buddha Eye*, pp. 22–30 and *Eastern Buddhist* 1:2 (1966), pp. 1–11.

66. Nishitani Keiji, *Kongenteki Shutaisei no Tetsugaku (Collected Writings)*, vols. 1 and 2.

67. Nishitani Keiji, *The Self-Overcoming of Nihilism*, trans. Graham Parkes with Setsuro Aihara (State University of New York Press, 1990).

68. Ibid., pp. 175, 179.

69. Nishitani, *Religion and Nothingness*, p. 32.

70. Ibid., p. 33.

71. Ibid., p. 93.

72. Ibid., pp. 85, 88.

73. Ibid., p. 90.

74. Ibid., pp. 96, 102.

75. Ibid., p. 131.

76. *Collected Writings*, vol. 11, p. 161.

77. *Kōza Tetsugaku Taikei* I, pp. 229–30.

78. Nishitani Keiji, "Science and Zen," trans. R. DeMartino, *Eastern Buddhist* 1:1 (1965), pp. 79–108; see Jan Van Bragt, "Religion and Science in Nishitani Keiji," *Buddhism Today* 5 (Kyoto, 1967), pp. 161–74.

79. "Science and Zen," p. 100.

80. Ibid., p. 107.

81. Nishitani Keiji, "The Significance of Zen in Modern Society," *Japanese Religions* 8:3 (1975), pp. 18–24; here p. 24.

82. *Die Gottesgeburt in der Seele und der Durchbruch zur Gottheit: Die Mystische Anthropologie Meister Eckharts und ihre Konfrontation mit der Mystik des Zen-Buddhismus* (Gütersloh, 1965); quotes, pp. 25, 34, 76, 101, 103, 119, 116, 118, 139, 140, 138, 146, 147, 169; see also "Der Zen-Buddhismus als 'Nicht-Mystik' under besonderer Berücksichtigung des Vergleichs zur Mystik Meister Eckharts," in *Transparente Welt*, ed. G. Schulz (Bern, Stuttgart, 1965), pp. 291–313. On Ueda see Buri, *Buddha-Christus*, 285–322.

83. He relies on the valuable work *Der Ochs und Sein Hirte*, trans. Koichi Tsujimura and Hartmut Buchner (Pfullingen: Neske, 1973), 2nd edition. There is an extensive literature concerning these pictures in Western languages.

84. Ueda Shizuteru, "Die Bewegung nach oben und die Bewegung nach unten: Zen Buddhismus im Vergleich mit Meister Eckhart," *Eranos-Jahrbuch 1981* (Frankfurt, 1982), pp. 223–72; quotes, pp. 230, 235, 259–61, 228, 243.

85. Ueda Shizuteru, "Nichijō Kūfu" ("Everyday Practice"), in the collection *Kōza Zen*, vol. 2 (Tokyo, 1974), pp. 146–75; quotations below, pp. 149–50.

86. See "Zen to Kotoba" (Zen and Language) and "Taiwa to Zen Mondō" (Dialogue and Zen Mondō) in Ueda's essay collection *Zen Buddhism* (Tokyo, 1973), pp. 65–133, 134–87; here pp. 135–36.

87. *Mumonkan* (see Chapter Three, note 9), cases eighteen and thirty-seven.

88. See Ueda, "'Nothingness' in Meister Eckhart and Zen Buddhism," in Franck, *Buddha Eye*, pp. 157–68; here pp. 164–66.

89. See Ueda, "Zen and Language," pp. 79ff.; Buri, *Buddha-Christus*, p. 311.

90.   Ueda, *Gottesgeburt*, p. 157.

91.   Ueda, "Zen and Language," pp. 68ff.

92.   Ueda, "Der Buddhismus und das Problem der Säkularisierung: Zur gegenwartigen geistigen Situation Japans," in *Hat Religion Zukunft?*, ed. Oskar Schatz (Graz, 1977), pp. 255–75; quotes, pp. 260–61, 268–69.

93.   *Nanzan Symposium 3: Zettai mu to kami* (Tokyo: Shunjūsha, 1981); see Jan Van Bragt's account of the symposium in Bulletin of the Nanzan Institute for Religion and Culture 5 (1980–81), pp. 29–47.

94.   See Toshihiko Izutsu, *Toward a Philosophy of Zen Buddhism* (Boulder, Colorado: Prajna Press, 1982). Izutsu deals in a modern way with philosophical themes of classical Zen Buddhism.

CHAPTER THREE

1.   On these developments see H. Dumoulin and John C. Maraldo, eds., *Buddhism in the Modern World* (New York: Collier; London: Macmillan, 1976).

2.   On the implantation of Buddhism in China see E. Zürcher, *The Buddhist Conquest of China*, rev. ed., 2 vols. (Leiden, 1972); H. Dumoulin, *Zen Buddhism: A History; Volume 1: India and China*, trans. James W. Heisig and Paul Knitter (New York: Macmillan, 1988).

3.   See, for example, the index to the colloquial words in the Tun-huang manuscripts, *Tonkō Hembunshu Kogo Goi Sakuin* (Kyoto, 1961).

4.   Ruth Fuller Sasaki, trans., *The Recorded Sayings of Ch'an Master Lin-chi Hui-chao of Chen Prefecture* (Kyoto, 1975).

5.   Paul Demiéville, *Entretiens de Lin-tsi* (Paris, 1972).

6.   Dumoulin, *History 1*, p. 172; see John Blofeld's translations, *The Zen Teaching of Hui Hai on Sudden Enlightenment* (London, 1962), and *The Zen Teaching of Huang Po* (London, 1958).

7. Ōhasami Shūei and August Faust, *Zen: Der Lebendige Buddhismus in Japan* (Gotha: Stuttgart, 1925).

8. *Bi-yän-lu: Meister Yüan-wu's Niederschrift von der Smaragdenen Felswand*, 3 vols. (Munich: Hanser, 1960–73).

9. See Thomas and J.C. Cleary, *The Blue Cliff Record*, 3 vols. (Boulder, Colorado: Shambhala, 1977) and Katsuki Sekida, *Two Zen Classics: Hekiganroku and Mumonkan* (New York, Tokyo, 1977).

10. Wu-men Hui-k'ai, *Wu-men-kuan: Zutritt nur durch die Wand* (Heidelberg, 1977).

11. Heinrich Dumoulin, *Mumonkan: Die Schranke ohne Tor, Meister Wu-men's Sammlung der 48 Koan* (Mainz, 1975).

12. Zenkei Shibayama, *Zen Comments on the Mumonkan* (San Francisco: Harper and Row, 1974); Kōun Yamada, *Gateless Gate* (Los Angeles: Center Publications, 1979).

13. *Nihon no Zen Goroku*, 20 vols. (Tokyo, 1977–78).

14. Collected sayings and letters translated by Philip Kapleau in *The Three Pillars of Zen* (Tokyo, 1965).

15. See James H. Sanford, *Zen-Man Ikkyū* (Chico, California: Scholars Press, 1981).

16. Musō Soseki, *Rinsen Kakun*, translation in Martin Collcutt, *Five Mountains* (Harvard University Press, 1981), pp. 149–65.

17. See D. T. Suzuki, *Zen and Japanese Culture* (Princeton University Press, 1959), pp. 95–115, 166–68.

18. Translations in *Eastern Buddhist* 3 (1970); 4 (1971); 8 (1975) and *Monumenta Nipponica* 6 (1943).

19. See Norman Waddell, trans., *The Unborn: The Life and Teaching of Zen Master Bankei, 1622–1693* (San Francisco, 1984).

20. See Philip Yampolsky, ed., *Zen Master Hakuin: Selected Writings* (New York, 1971); Trevor Leggett, *A Second Zen Reader* (Tokyo: Tuttle, 1988), pp. 129–56.

21. Bibliography in H. Dumoulin, *Zen Buddhism: A History; Volume 2: Japan*, pp. 467–68, and the notes to the sections on individual masters.

22. Dieter Schwaller, *Der Japanische Ōbaku-Mönch Tetsugen Dōkō*: Leben, Denken, Schriften (Bern, 1989).

23. See also Dumoulin, *History 2*, pp. 51–119.

24. Norman Waddell and Masao Abe, trans., *The Eastern Buddhist* 6:2, pp. 115–28; German translation by H. Dumoulin, *Monumenta Nipponica*, 14 (1958), pp. 429–36; revised in *Dōgen Zen* (Munich: Theseus, 1990), pp. 37–45. For what follows see Carl Bielefeldt, *Dōgen's Manuals of Zen Meditation* (University of California Press, 1988).

25. See the German articles of R.K. Heinemann, "Zokugo in Dōgen's *Shōbōgenzō*," *Oriens Extremus* 15 (1968), pp. 101–19, 179–90; 16 (1969), pp. 169–79; 18 (1971), pp. 67–83.

26. Kōsen Nishiyama and John Stevens, *Shōbōgenzō*, 4 vols. (Tokyo: Hakayama Shobo, 1975, 1977, 1983). Another complete English translation has recently appeared: Yūhō Yokoi, *The Shōbōgenzō*, 5 vols. (Tokyo: Sankibo, 1986).

27. See the bibliography in Dumoulin, *History 2*, p. 475.

28. D.T. Suzuki, *Essays in Zen Buddhism: First Series*, essay four.

29. See their exchange in *Philosophy East and West* 3 (1953) and in D. T. Suzuki, *Studies in Zen* (London: Rider, 1955) pp. 129–64.

30. See Nukariya Kaiten, *The Religion of the Samurai: A Study of Zen Philosophy and Discipline in China and Japan* (London, 1913), one of the earliest books on Zen in a Western language. This important scholar also published a two-volume work in Japanese on the history of Zen (Tokyo, 1923).

31. For the text, see Dumoulin, *History 1*, p. 87; for the Bodhidharma legend, see pp. 83–90.

32. Bernard Faure describes this biography as "fairly authentic" in his article "Bodhidharma," in *The Encyclopedia of Religion* (New York, London, 1987), vol. II, p. 263.

33. His most important works are listed in Dumoulin, *History 2*, p. 471.

34. For the present state of research on Bodhidharma see Bernard Faure, *Le Traité de Bodhidharma: Traduction et Commentaire* (Paris: Le Mail, 1986); he assesses the fundamental contributions of Suzuki and Yanagida and gives a full bibliography of the sources and secondary literature.

35. See David W. Chappell, "The Teachings of the Fourth Ch'an Patriarch Tao- hsin (580–651)," in *Early Ch'an in China and Tibet*, ed. Whalen Lai and Lewis R. Lancaster (Berkeley: University of California Press, 1983), pp. 89–106; here p. 94. An English translation of the text attributed to Tao-hsin is appended, pp. 107–29.

36. See John R. McRae, *The Northern School and the Formation of Early Ch'an Buddhism* (Honolulu: University of Hawaii Press, 1986), chapter six, "The Basic Doctrines of the East Mountain Teaching," pp. 118–47; a translation of this text appears on pp. 121–32.

37. Dumoulin, *History 1*, p. 100.

38. McRae, *Northern School*, p. 143; also in Chappell, "Teachings of the Fourth Patriarch," p. 110.

39. McRae, *Northern School*, p. 123.

40. Ibid., p. 122.

41. Ibid., p. 125.

42. Ibid., p. 134.

43. Ibid., p. 135.

44. Ibid.

45. Ibid., p. 136.

46. Ibid., p. 132.

47. Ibid., p. 142.

48. See Bielefeldt, *Dōgen's Manuals*.

49. McRae, *Northern School*, gives a comprehensive and well-documented account. See also Lai and Lancaster, *Early Ch'an;* Bernard Faure, *La Volonté d'Orthodoxie dans le Bouddhisme Chinois* (Paris, 1988); Robert M. Gimello and Peter N. Gregory, eds., *Studies in Ch'an and Hua-yen* (Honolulu, 1983).

50. Traditional dates (670–762) corrected in light of the discovery of his funerary stele (Faure, *Traité de Bodhidharma*, p. 7).

51. On the origin of the terms "Northern school" and "East Mountain teaching," see McRae, *Northern School*, pp. 8–10.

52. On Shen-hsiu's death and burial, see McRae, *Northern School*, pp. 54–56, with a translation of the *Memorial* by Sung Chih-wen, pp. 52–53.

53. Chih-ta also studied with Shen-hsiu; important sections from his writing on sudden enlightenment, "Tun-wu yao-chüeh," are presented in Faure, *La Volonté d'Orthodoxie*, pp. 182ff.

54. The writing of Hsüan-tse is not extant. The *Ryōga Shijiki* is a chronicle of the first half of the eighth century; see McRae, *Northern School*, pp. 88–91, and Dumoulin, *History 1*, pp. 109–10.

55. McRae, *Northern School*, p. 65.

56. Ibid., pp. 56–71.

57. Paul Demiéville has translated the acts of the Council of Lhasa from Chinese with a commentary; see his *Choix d'études Bouddhiques* (Leiden, 1973).

58. See McRae, *Northern School*, p. 70.

59. See John McRae, "The Ox-head School of Chinese Ch'an," in Gimello and Gregory, *Studies in Ch'an and Hua-yen*, pp. 169–252; Dumoulin, *History 1*, pp. 115–17.

60. See Dumoulin, *History 2*, pp. 7–14; B. Faure, "The Daruma-shu, Dōgen, and Sōtō Zen," *Monumenta Nipponica* 42 (1987), pp. 25–55.

61. Biographical details in Dumoulin, *History 2*, pp. 42–43.

62. Ibid., pp. 69–71, 122, 127.

63. See, for example, the "diagnostic history" of the Buddha in W. Lange-Eichbaum, *Genie, Irrsinn und Ruhm* (Munich, 1935), p. 360.

64. See Katsuki Sekida, *Zen Training: Methods and Philosophy* (New York, Tokyo: Weatherhill, 1975).

65. Karlfried Graf Dürckheim, *Hara: Die Erdmitte des Menschen* (Weilheim, 1967), p. 125.

66. Nyanaponika Thera, *The Heart of Buddhist Meditation* (London: Rider, 1962).

67. See Tomo Hirai, *Zen and the Mind* (Tokyo: Japan Publications, 1978).

68. William Johnston, *Silent Music: The Science of Meditation* (New York, Evanston, San Francisco: Harper and Row, 1974), pp. 29–30.

69. Suzuki, *An Introduction to Zen Buddhism* (London: Rider, 1969), pp. 9– 29.

70. Suzuki, *Essays in Zen Buddhism: Second Series* (London: Rider, 1970), pp. 31–39); compare to William James, *Varieties of Religious Experience* (New York: Modern Library, 1936), pp. 371–72.

71. Translated in Mircea Eliade, *Yoga: Immortality and Freedom* (Princeton University Press, 1969), pp. 123–24.

72. See Nakamura Hajime, *Shin Bukkyo Jiten* (Tokyo, 1962), p. 13.

73. C.G. Carus, *Psyche: Zur Entwicklungsgeschichte der Seele* (1846; recently reprinted).

74. Suzuki, *An Introduction*, pp. 21–22.

75. Ibid., p. 15.

76. Fromm et al., *Zen Buddhism and Psychoanalysis*, p. 116.

77. D. T. Suzuki, *Zen Buddhism* (New York: Doubleday, 1956), p. 3; quoted by Fromm et al., p. 116.

78. Fromm et al., pp. 116–17.

79. Ibid., pp. 121, 123.

80. Ibid., p. 139.

81. Suzuki, *Essays in Zen Buddhism: Second Series*, p. 36.

82. James, *Varieties of Religious Experience*, p. 506.

83. Johnston, *Silent Music*, p. 116.

84. See Bruno Rhyner, *Morita-Psychotherapie und Zen-Buddhismus* (Zürich, 1988), p. 35. This book, which I am following here, has an appendix of statistical tables and a comprehensive bibliography.

85. Hirai, *Zen and the Mind*, refers to a questionnaire in which 22 of the respondents found similarities with Zen and 21 did not. Rhyner gives a number of similar judgments from Japanese doctors and psychologists. In *The Encyclopedia of Religion* (New York, London: Macmillan, 1987) vol. 12, p. 64, James Heisig offers the judgment that "the influence of Zen is evident." Satō Kōji, professor of psychology at Kyoto University, has dealt with the Morita therapy in a series of articles in the international psychological review *Psychologia* between 1958 and 1965. The close relation between Morita therapy and Zen is defended by Usa Genyū and his son, Usa Shin'ichi, and by Morita's pupil, Suzuki Tomonori. According to the American psychologist, David K. Reynolds, the overlap between the theoretical and methodical orientation of Morita therapy and Zen is great enough to substantiate an intellectual dependence of Morita on Zen; in *Morita-Psychology* (Berkeley and Los Angeles, 1976), as quoted in Rhyner, *Morita- Psychotherapie*, p. 47.

86. Quoted in Rhyner, *Morita-Psychotherapie*, p. 35.

87. See Rhyner, *Morita-Psychotherapie*, pp. 54–65, 71–87.

88. Ibid., p. 59.

CHAPTER FOUR

1. See *Shōbōgenzō Zuimonki* (a text drawn up by Dōgen's disciple Ejō), II 26; trans. Masunaga Reihō, *A Primer of Sōtō Zen* (Honolulu, 1971), p. 47.

2. See the description of Paul Imhof, "Nach unten und nach oben. Eine Grundbewegung des Leibes," *Geist und Leben* 61 (1988), pp. 229ff.

3. *The Spiritual Exercises of St. Ignatius Loyola*, trans. Thomas Corbishley (Wheathampstead, Hertfordshire, 1979), p. 85.

4. Hanna-Barbara Gerl, *Romani Guardini 1898-1968: Leben und Werk* (Mainz, 1985), p. 209.

5. Romano Guardini, *Wille und Wahrheit* (Mainz, 1933), first ed., pp. 13, 19, 44, 70, 73, 120, 122.

6. In the introduction to her biography Gerl writes: "The search for the essential led him at times to take an interest in the figure of the Buddha, though this left scarcely any trace in written form" (pp. 12–13). For the 1937–38 winter semester he planned a course on "The Death of the Buddha: The Buddhist interpretation of the meaning of existence and the understanding of Christianity" (ibid., p. 281). "One type of lecture course dealt with figures in cultural history covering an astonishingly wide span from Socrates to Rilke, and even reaching out to the Buddha" (ibid., p. 283).

7. Ichirō Okumura, *Erwachen zu Gott: Stimme aus dem Karmel in Japan* (Munich, 1976), p. 47.

8. Shunryū Suzuki, *Zen Mind, Beginner's Mind* (New York, Tokyo: Weatherhill, 1970), p. 25.

9. See Bielefeldt, *Dōgen's Manuals*, p. 181.

10. Quoted in Dumoulin, *History 2*, p. 77; see the accompanying explanation and note 116 on p. 113.

11. Klaus Riesenhuber, "Zum Verständnis ungegenständlicher Meditation," *Internationale katholische Zeitschrift*, 15 (1986), pp. 321ff.

12. Suzuki, *Zen Mind, Beginner's Mind*, p. 43, and the section on "no duality," pp. 42–45.

13. Riesenhuber, "Zum Verständnis," p. 322.

14. Gregory of Nyssa, *De Vita Moysis*, PG 44, pp. 376–77.

15. Richard of Saint-Victor, *Benjamin Major*, I 6; *Benjamin Minor*, 71, 72; the two texts are found in Migne, *Patrologia Latina*, vol. 196, cols. 1–202. See Heinrich Dumoulin, *Östliche Meditation und Christliche Mystik* (Freiburg, Munich, 1966), pp. 169–88.

16. *The Spiritual Exercises*, p. 112.

17. Riesenhuber, "Zum Verständnis," p. 325.

18. See the accounts in three books of the Harada line of Zen Buddhism (Tokyo 1956, 1959, 1962) briefly reviewed in Heinrich Dumoulin, *Zen Enlightenment: Origins and Meanings*, trans. John Maraldo (New York, Tokyo: Weatherhill, 1979), pp. 125–53. See also the many quotations in my contribution to the Horst Hammitzsche Festschrift (Wiesbaden, 1971): "Selbstzeugnisse Japanischer Zen-Jünger über die seelische Haltungen während der Zen-Meditation," pp. 85–102.

19. Otto Faust, ed., *Zen—der lebendige Buddhismus in Japan: Ausge-wählte Stücke des Zen-Textes*, translated and introduced by Shūei Ōhasama, with a preface by Rudolf Otto (Gotha and Stuttgart, 1925).

20. Douglas R. Hofstadter, *Gödel, Escher, Bach: An Eternal Golden Braid* (New York: Basic Books, 1979), chapter one. There are several further references to koans in chapters ten and eleven.

21. See Jörg Röttgen, "Die Romane des Zen-Kriminalisten," *Publik-Forum* 22 (November 3, 1989), pp. 20–24.

22. See Ruth Fuller Sasaki's excellent study of the history of the koan in Rinzai- Zen, in Isshū Miura and Ruth Fuller Sasaki, eds., *The Zen Koan* (Kyoto, 1965), pp. 3–32.

23. Miura and Sasaki, *The Zen Koan*, p. 10.

24. D.T. Suzuki, *Essays in Zen Buddhism* II (London: Rider, 1970), pp. 90–91.

25. Miura and Sasaki, *The Zen Koan*, p. 7.

26. Sekida, *Two Zen Classics*, p. 28.

27. Miura and Sasaki, *The Zen Koan*, p. xi.

28. Izutsu, *Toward a Philosophy of Zen Buddhism*, p. 176.

29. William Johnston, *The Mirror Mind: Spirituality and Transformation* (London: Collins, 1981), p. 97.

30. William Johnston, *Christian Zen* (Harper and Row, 1971), pp. 61–62; Johnston suggests many possible Christian koans in this chapter, pp. 57–67. Kakichi Kadowaki's book *Zen and the Bible* (Penguin Arkana, 1990), illustrates with numerous examples the remarkable affinity he notes between Scripture and koans.

31. Wilhelm Gundert, explaining the forty-first case in the *Bi-yän-lu* (Japanese: *Hekiganroku*) (Munich, 1986), p. 123.

32. *Thomas Merton on Zen* (London, 1976), p. 108.

33. Johnston, *Christian Zen*, p. 62.

34. See the full presentation in Kadowaki's recent Japanese book: *Invitation to Meditation: Linking East and West* (Tokyo, 1989), pp. 175–80; quotation, p. 176.

35. *Thomas Merton on Zen*, p. 86.

36. D. T. Suzuki, *An Introduction to Zen Buddhism* (London: Rider, 1969), p. 95.

37. Ibid., p. 93.

38. Shibayama, *Zen Comments on the Mumonkan*, pp. 25–27, 29.

39. See his commentary on the *Mumonkan* in *Mumonkan Teishō* (Tokyo, 1957), p. 9.

40. *Experiences of Enlightenment in Zen* (in Japanese, Tokyo, 1959), pp. 288–89.

41. Yves Raguin, "Christian Spirituality and Spiritualities of Other Religions," *Bulletin of the Secretariatus pro non-Christianis* 23 (1988), pp. 152–53.

42. Enomiya-Lassalle, *Zen und christliche Mystik* (Freiburg, 1986), p. 486.

43. Ibid., p. 488.

44. Raguin, "Christian Spirituality," pp. 152–53.

45. See especially Romano Guardini, *Theologische Briefe an einen Freund* (Munich, Paderborn, Vienna, 1976), letter 6: "Teilhard de Chardin as symptom," pp. 46–49.

46. See Henri de Lubac, *La Pensée Religieuse du Père Teilhard de Chardin* (Paris, 1962).

47. Case nineteen, Sekida, *Two Zen Classics*, p. 73.

48. See Jan Van Bragt, *Bulletin of the Nanzan Institute for Religion and Culture* 4, pp. 8–18; pp. 10–23.

49. *Bulletin of the Nanzan Institute* 4, p. 18. During their audience on September 9, 1987, the Pope encouraged the Buddhist participants with these words: "Through the attentive listening and the mutual respect which characterize these exchanges interreligious dialogue can reach an increasingly more profound level. At the previous intermonastic exchange, the Christian monks who lived at your monasteries had the occasion to appreciate your time-honored traditions. They were very moved by your fraternal hospitality. I wish to thank you for your exquisite courtesy and I would hope that such encounters will continue in the future." (*Bulletin of the Secretariatus pro non-Christianis* 23 [1988], p. 5).

INDEX

ABOUT THE AUTHORS

HEINRICH DUMOULIN holds a Ph.D. from the Gregorian University, Rome; a D. Litt. from the University of Tokyo; and an honorary Doctorate in Theology from the University of Würzburg. A resident of Tokyo since 1935, he was Professor of Philosophy and History of Religions at Sophia University in Tokyo from 1941 to 1976. His writings include *Kamo Mabuchi: Ein Beitrag zur japanischen Religions- und Geistesgeschichte* (Tokyo, 1943); *The Development of Chinese Zen After the Sixth Patriarch* (New York, 1953); *Zen Geschichte und Gestalt* (Bern, 1959), translated as *A History of Zen Buddhism* (New York, 1963); *Östliche Meditation und christliche Mystik* (Freiburg, 1966); editor, *Buddhismus der Gegenwart* (Freiburg, 1970), translated as *Buddhism in the Modern World* (New York, 1976); *Christianity Meets Buddhism* (La Salle, Illinois, 1974); *Zen Englightenment* (Tokyo, 1979); and many works in the Japanese language.

JOSEPH S. O'LEARY, an Irish theologian, lectures in the Department of English Literature, Sophia University. He is the author of *Questioning Back: The Overcoming of Metaphysics in Christian Tradition* (New York: Harper & Row) and *La Recherche du Relatif: Essai sur la Texture Pluraliste du Christianisme* (forthcoming).

The "weathermark" identifies this book as a production of Weatherhill, Inc., publishers of fine books on Asia and the Pacific. Editorial supervision: Pam Cook. Typography, book and cover design: Liz Trovato. Production supervision: Bill Rose. Typesetting: Tenth Avenue Editions, New York. Printing and binding R.R. Donnelley, Harrisonburg, Virginia.